SPIRIT INCORPORATED

SPIRIT INCORPORATED

How to Follow Your Spiritual Path
From 9 to 5

KATHLEEN HAWKINS

DeVorss Publications

ISBN: 0-87516-717-9

Library of Congress Catalog Card Number 98-70371

Parts of this book have appeared
in *Science of Mind*, *Unity*, and *Success* magazines.

Chapter 14 is dedicated to my friends Maggie and Garvin

DeVorss & Company, *Publishers*
Box 550
Marina del Rey CA 90294

Printed in the United States of America

Dedicated to
CHARLES PATRICK WADE JONES

with special thanks to
DeEtte Gwendolyn Hawkins
and Charlene Wade Groom
for their encouragement

Spirit is the life-giving, animating force within all things, the real essence and significance of something.

To be spiritual means to seek, sense, and honor this inner presence.

To do your job, or conduct business, 'consciously' means to:

1. Know 'right' (what's most life-affirming) from 'wrong' (what's obtained at the expense of others or to their detriment).

2. Realize how your actions, attitudes, choices, and decisions affect others.

3. Act for the greatest good of all involved.

Contents

An Invitation to Work with 'Upper' Management

WHAT'S THE bottom line in business? Many people would answer, 'Money' or 'Profit.' There are growing numbers of us, however, who answer differently. We believe that the real bottom line in business is spiritual and personal growth.

We believe there's a Power greater than we are that's within all things and always active in business. This Spirit, which is absolute on a universal level, is relative on the human level and is expressed individually through each of us.

Since you're a personalized expression of this greater Power, you can use it to improve every aspect of your life, including the time you spend at the office. The extent to which you recognize this Power and access it is the extent to which your life works for you. In the workplace this perspective helps you to:

- express yourself more creatively
- demonstrate higher ideals, values, and ethics
- manifest continuing prosperity and wealth
- value employees, management, customers, clients, and yourself

Using universal principles at work gives your spiritual life a nuts-'*n*'-bolts practicality. What better place to practice your faith than at the office, where you probably spend at least eight hours a day, five days a week.

As the business world becomes more complex and demanding, you may be looking for a strong, significant foundation on which to build your professional life, job, or career. *Spirit Incorporated* invites you to do this by exploring your own relationship with a universal Power, whether you call it 'Higher Self,' 'Life,' 'Inner Self,' 'Good,' or 'God,' or some other name. This book shows you exactly how to write a mission statement that reflects your highest ideals, gives you practical ideas on how to express yourself in more positive ways, and invites you to renew your faith in yourself and others. It shares more than 200 exciting ideas that you can use to free your inner spiritual genius, contribute something of value to others, and keep in touch with 'Upper/Inner' Management, your source of inspiration.

Spiritual Laws Operating in the Workplace

We are one with Life because we are created *from* it. Ernest Holmes said it well when he compared our union with the Whole to drops of water in the ocean: "While a drop of water is not the ocean . . . it does contain within itself all the attributes of the limitless deep." The Bible likewise reinforces this insight by declaring that we are made in the image and likeness of God. And now quantum physics confirms the fundamental oneness of the universe by saying that everything—visible and invisible—is a form of the same energy. Each of us, then, being composed of matter (visible energy) and thought (invisible energy), is created from this one 'entity.' It's the Spirit that animates us and gives us life.

This Life Force operates according to certain universal laws.

If you work *with* these laws instead of against them and act for the highest good of all involved, your daily experiences will take on a spiritual, life-affirming quality. This book shows you how to use the following principles to turn every day at the office into a powerful spiritual workshop.

Unity

Just as you're an expression of the one universal Energy, business is also part of the universe and is spiritual in nature. When you realize this, you can use spiritual laws to increase your job satisfaction, improve your working relationships, multiply your income or profit, and build a cooperative consciousness with others.

Cause and Effect

Thought—fueled by feelings—acting on Energy leads to action. This in turn produces the effect, the outward experience. The steps to signing a contract, for example, or finding the 'right' job or increasing your earning power all begin in your mind with a thought. The quality of your thoughts affects the quality of your experiences. When you conduct business consciously—with honesty, integrity, and a spirit of cooperation—your life tends to get better and the lives of others are enhanced for doing business with you.

Attraction: Like Attracts Like

What you think about on a regular basis often appears in your outward experience. If you're fearful or suspicious, for example, and believe that people are out to get you, that'll probably happen. If you believe, however, that there's a power for good that operates through all things and you work with confidence, your life at the office will run more smoothly. And if you're faced with challenges, as most of us are in the workplace, you'll be more relaxed, creative, and resourceful.

Circulation

Energy is always in motion, always in circulation—Life in full, abundant expression. You risk interfering with the flow of this vibrant Energy if you engage in less than life-affirming behavior, the biggest of which is fear—fear of loss or lack: the root of every 'negative' emotion. When you're fearful, you postpone more good from coming into your life.

Release

To keep the Life Energy flowing, release your fears and affirm a belief in abundance: abundance of wealth, ideas, solutions, and answers. The way to affirm abundance is to share your talent, money, and knowledge. This asserts the reality that there's more where that came from.

Resurrection

Energy is neither created nor destroyed, only *transformed*. This is good to remember in business, especially if times get tough. Many of us spend a lot of time acquiring money, accounts, clients, promotions, and prestige. We're geared up to 'get and gain,' but if we're in business long enough, we may encounter difficult challenges such as downsizing, personality conflicts, a stock market correction, or a 'bad' investment.

If you remember the Law of Resurrection, you realize that the one Life that permeates everything is a constant, regardless of the various forms the outward conditions take. And you can use this knowledge to maintain your equilibrium, recover faster from apparent losses or difficulties, and reinvest your creativity in order to achieve something as good as you had or better.

Welcome to a New Way of Working

This book is for you if you want to do your job more consciously by acting on your personal relationship with 'Upper' Management, or 'Inner' Management, as you understand it. If you decide to choose life-affirming alternatives over the traditional warfare model of doing business, you'll discover that when you put people and principles before profit, success comes naturally. And each day at the office becomes a fulfilling spiritual experience.

Chapter 1

HELP WANTED

Someone to express love, wisdom, and prosperity in creative, unique ways

Salary: top of the scale

Benefits: excellent

Opportunities for advancement: excellent

Apply: within

LET'S ASSUME for a moment that long before your first job you were hired for another job, for something greater and more global than 'nine-to-five.' You were employed by Life to:

1. Enjoy continuing love and prosperity
2. Live creatively with enthusiasm

3. Use a life-affirming perspective in everything you do
4. Contribute something of value to others and to society
5. Continue to evolve spiritually

Would that affect the way you do your job or conduct business? Would it influence your approach to your profession or your career? Imagine, at least for the length of this book, that it's true there is a spiritual foundation to the universe. Then watch what happens. You may find that as you apply a life-affirming perspective at the office, you begin to enjoy greater job satisfaction, more enthusiasm, and better working relationships. And if you're faced with challenging situations such as mergers, a hard day at the office, bankruptcy, personality conflicts, or ever-changing marketplaces, you'll be more creative and more confident dealing with them.

In-Company Hiring

No outsiders were considered for the job of being yourself—an individualized expression of the universe—because there is no outside. We're all created from the same Energy and therefore we belong to the same 'company,' of which each of us is an integral part.

There weren't any résumés to write and no palm-sweating interviews to endure to get the job. You got it because you're related to the president of the company—the Infinite.

A computer instructor once said of choosing a spiritual life, "It's like making the decision to go into a warm, well-lit, friendly store after having stood outside in the cold looking in."

Personally, I believe that you're *already inside* the warm, well-lit store. That friendly store is all there is, all there has ever been, and all there ever will be. You're already inside! All you have to do is open your eyes and awaken to that fact.

Salary: Top of the Scale
Benefits: Excellent

Because you're on Life's bankroll, your earning power is infinite, benefits are plentiful, and every day is payday. Your salary and benefits include family, friends, creative ideas, opportunities, insights, and personal growth. A paycheck is only one source of your supply.

You may have noticed that some people seem to receive a better 'income' in life than others. They're richer, happier, and more fulfilled. What do they do differently? They remember to pick up their paychecks by having faith in themselves, appreciating what they've already earned, working with confidence and integrity, and expecting the best. Have you picked up *your* paycheck yet? Today is payday. *Every* day is payday.

What Product Do You Manufacture?

A business produces material goods or services. The products of your spiritual life are your attitudes, thoughts, words, and actions. Because it's your inherent nature as a human being to be enterprising and your thoughts are automatically creative, you're always producing something. It would be in your best interest, then, if you want to have a good life, to produce positive products—joy, happiness, and peace of mind—for yourself and others.

An Open Door Policy

You have direct access to universal Love, Wisdom, and Intelligence because you are created from it, just as the 'single' drop of water is part of the greater ocean, the waters of Life; or the 'individual' flame is part of the greater fire, the divine Fire. To make the most of this opportunity, stay in touch with 'Upper' Management, your Higher/Inner Self, by meditating or praying regularly, reading inspiring material, and thinking about the continuing role of Spirit at the office.

When you meet regularly with Upper Management, you'll find answers to your questions more quickly, solve problems faster, feel better about yourself, make wiser decisions, and reconfirm that you're working on the right priorities. So talk to the Boss any time. The door is always open. Go on in.

Desperation Is a Form of Atheism, Confidence a Form of Faith

When you realize that you were originally hired by Life to express life-affirming qualities on earth, you'll realize that even if you're between jobs or between bank accounts, you're still employed.

Maria was looking desperately for a teaching job. She flooded the market with résumés and had gone on countless interviews. She confided, "My ego was taking such a beating. I began to wonder if I was worthy of the job I wanted. Why was it taking so long to be hired?

"Then one day I realized that I was giving prospective employers the power to determine my self-worth. I took it personally if they didn't hire me and, consequently, felt terrible about myself. I finally understood that my desperation was a form of atheism. When I became discouraged, I wasn't trusting that things would work out ultimately for the best. I'd been setting in motion a self-fulfilling prophecy of disappointment.

"I began to affirm that I had an even more important job to do than work for any particular school system. That job was to deepen my understanding of my relationship with Life. When I understood this and began to live accordingly, things turned around. With my sense of self-worth restored, I was more confident in interviews. A short time later I was offered the perfect job, which I gladly accepted.''

Apply Within

There's virtually no commute for the job of being yourself—no traffic jams, no red lights, no flat tires, no honking horns. Simply close your eyes, take a couple of deep, cleansing breaths, and let the power of the Life within energize you, the presence of Life nurture you, and the intelligence of Life guide you.

Quiet Time

For many of us spirituality is a private, personal matter, which might seem odd to think about at work. But even in the workplace your faith can be a subtle, powerful force that you can comfortably and discreetly integrate into your job or career.

But the workplace is full of noise, demands and deadlines, ringing telephones, people wanting things, and countless interruptions—all of which can interfere with your work. It's because of all this 'busyness' that it's crucial to allow yourself some quiet time throughout the day. This will help you collect your thoughts even if it's just to sit quietly for a moment at your desk before beginning your next assignment or to arrive a few minutes early to a meeting.

Kenneth Thurston Hurst, one-time president of the publishing company Prentice-Hall International, comments that:

Divine higher power exists all around us, and we have only to plug into it—to make the God-connection. In addition to coffee breaks, I think we should take God breaks and the most effective way is through meditation. Meditation involves getting quiet and allowing the higher self—what Emerson calls the Oversoul and Paul Brunton calls the Overself—to take over.

Mr. Hurst says that he was responsible for having a meditation room installed at Prentice-Hall:

We called it a Quiet Room and people could sit there peacefully when they felt too much stress from the telephones and their co-workers. It's helpful to take a mental retreat for five or ten minutes, then go back to the phones and do a better job, and also feel refreshed.

Another way to create quiet time at work is to make appointments with yourself, during which time you can pray or meditate. If people want to meet with you at that time, simply tell them that you have an appointment. Then when you return to work, you'll feel renewed, better able to concentrate, and prepared to give people the attention they deserve.

You could also create some undisturbed time by telling people the best time to call you. Naturally, it'll be a time other than when you're on your break or concentrating on high-priority items, which for most people is in the morning.

One morning at nine o'clock I called the editorial offices of *Science of Mind* magazine, a publication dedicated to exploring and teaching spiritual principles. I was surprised and pleased to have a recording tell me that the staff was in daily meditation until 9:30. What a great way to start the day! They were also putting their philosophy to use and setting a good example for callers.

Another time I called a large insurance company in the morning and was told that the first hour of each business day was the employees' 'quiet hour,' the time during which they can work undisturbed on their high-payoff items. An excellent idea and, I might add, a great opportunity for the spiritually inclined to do some deep breathing, relax after their morning commute, and say an affirmation for a productive day.

Business environments today are becoming more humane. The American Institute of Architects in Washington, D.C., notes a definite trend toward worker-friendly buildings. The Institute's studies show that when workers feel more at ease in their offices, they are more productive—and, incidentally, more able to get in touch with themselves spiritually.

Increasing numbers of companies are providing fitness centers, tracks for running, or swimming pools for their people, realizing that healthy employees work better and reduce health insurance premiums. If you're fortunate enough to work for one of these companies, consider using these activities as 'moving meditations' to make that higher connection or to reflect on how well you're using spiritual principles.

Because of all the demands in business that can distract or overwhelm you, it's essential to keep in touch with your inner guidance. You'll find it in the silences that you regularly create for yourself during the day.

Opportunities for Advancement

Every day you have opportunities to advance spiritually. Here are six ideas on how you might progress through an ideal day:

1. Before you go to work, you remind yourself of your true job description: to express love, wisdom, and prosperity in creative, unique ways. You keep this in mind during the day and you stay positive, focused, and on target.

2. You visit 'Upper' Management, or 'Inner' Management, throughout the day, whether sitting quietly for a moment at your desk or replacing one of your breaks with a meditation or a prayer break.

3. Before you begin each assignment, you take a moment to breathe deeply so you can think clearly and concentrate comfortably on the task at hand.

4. If you're the boss or owner of the company, you provide a pleasant, quiet room where people can go if they need time to be by themselves.

5. After interruptions, you quickly restore your concentration by taking a deep breath and repeating a word or phrase to yourself until you feel your focus returning to the task at hand. This could be a mantra or any word or phrase that has a calming effect on you, such as *peace*, *tranquillity*, *success*, or your own name.

6. At the end of the day, you reflect on the spiritual products you manufactured that day: thoughts, words, feelings, attitudes. If you were less than happy, analyze what went wrong and tomorrow begin anew.

Life-Long Employment

The job of expressing love, wisdom, and abundance in creative ways is yours as long as you want it. You have seniority. No one is better at being you than *you* are. You have no rivals, no competition. The universe is forever unfolding uniquely through you. Every situation at work is an opportunity to explore your beliefs about prosperity and life and to make a personal statement about those beliefs. Because you're part of creation, you are valuable. You play a vital, far-reaching role in the universe. You are needed. You got the job. Congratulations!

■

"Begin where you are. It would be unscientific to begin anywhere else."

Ernest Holmes, The Science of Mind

■

"There is a guidance for each of us, and by lowly listening we shall hear the right word. . . . Place yourself in the middle of the stream of power and wisdom which flows into your life. Then, without effort, you are impelled to truth and to perfect contentment."

Ralph Waldo Emerson

■

"To improve the golden moment of opportunity and catch the good that is within our reach, is the great art of life."

Samuel Johnson

■

"To love oneself is the beginning of a lifelong romance."

Oscar Wilde

■

"Some very wonderful things happen when a person succeeds in knowing what is basic and essential . . ."

The Great Religions by Which Men Live *(Hinduism)*

■

Chapter 2

Mission Possible: What's Yours?

How to Write a Mission Statement to Inspire and Motivate Yourself

IMAGINE WAKING up every day refreshed, in a positive state of mind, and excited about going to work. Imagine staying on target all day, meeting challenges from a spiritual perspective, and ending each day with a sense of accomplishment. All this is possible when you have a mission statement that reflects your spiritual outlook.

A company develops a mission statement so the various departments within the organization can budget their resources, better focus their activities to achieve the company's objectives, and work toward a common goal.

As the chief executive officer of your *own* life, you have a wonderful opportunity to create a mission statement for your professional life that addresses your deepest values. But how exactly do you write one? Here are some ideas.

The Theme

Most successful mission statements revolve around the following theme: to earn a living or make a profit and feel fulfilled while contributing to others by providing quality products.

Variations on the Theme

Now choose the phrases below to tailor a mission statement for yourself that fits your values, or use the phrases to generate your own ideas. Feel free to change the order of the items. As you draft your statement, keep in mind that it is spiritually correct to be rich, provided you do it ethically. That is, after all, one of the reasons you're in business or have a job—to make money.

It's my mission (or my company's mission)
. . . to be well paid (or make a good profit)
(to create a financially healthy company, make an excellent
living, live comfortably, prosper financially, wisely
manage my resources or the company's resources,
be an example of prosperity,
manifest abundance for myself and others)

. . . for doing work
(name your profession or service)

. . . that enriches
(inspires, fulfills, motivates, satisfies,
spiritually supports)

me (or us)
. . . and contributes something of value to others
(that inspires people, helps them improve the quality
of their lives, makes a positive difference, serves
customers and clients well, promotes harmony,
comforts people, values employees, gives people hope,
supports innovation and creativity, rewards teamwork,
helps the environment, improves health care,
serves the community)

. . . by providing a quality product or service
(name your product or service)

Sample Mission Statements

The following mission statements exemplify many of the ideas above.

Business Ethics magazine (Minneapolis, Minn.)

To promote ethical business practices, to serve that growing community of professionals striving to live and work in responsible ways, and to create a financially healthy company in the process.

Craft Marketing Connections (Ireton, Iowa)

To provide clients with enthusiastic, reliable service and the best quality product possible while creating a positive working environment in which company members take pride in their work based on faith in themselves.

Kathleen Hawkins, Vice President
National Management Institute (Flower Mound, Tex.)

To express my evolving spirituality through my speaking and writing and, in doing so, to prosper financially and to inspire others and support them in their personal growth and spiritual unfoldment.

New Leaders Press (San Francisco, Calif.)

To encourage and support the full expression of the human spirit and the evolution of consciousness in the business community.

NLP Learning Systems Corporation (Dallas, Tex.)

To promote world peace through better communication,
to teach success through language, to increase holographic
thinking and to be a living example of prosperity.

Science of Mind magazine (Los Angeles, Calif.)

To demonstrate that Divine Spirit is the ultimate truth
of all being, and that by drawing upon that Power and
using it intelligently, we can enjoy meaningful,
prosperous, and fulfilling lives.

How to Keep Your Mission in Mind

To avoid the out-of-sight/out-of-mind syndrome, keep your mission statement close at hand throughout the day—on your desk or in your purse, briefcase, or wallet. Or use your computer to help you. If you have a screen-saver program that darkens your monitor after so many minutes of non-use, consider programming it to scroll your guiding principles across the screen. If you have a daily-reminder program, have it display your mission statement at the beginning of each day or display affirmations to keep you on target such as:

- I have peace, poise, and power
- I make excellent money doing work I love
- I expect the best and receive what I want or better

You could also keep some item in your office that reminds you of your mission as it relates to your personal values. Be creative. I know an entrepreneur with an office in her home who has a small stained-glass church sitting on her desk to remind her to keep a spiritual perspective; another businessperson who keeps a picture of a lighthouse in her office; a woman who works in a doctor's office who contributed an angelfish to the office aquarium. If you want to go the angelfish route, though, be sure that angelfish are compatible with the other breeds already in the aquarium!

If you're the boss, you might have the company's mission statement printed on your newsletter, brochure, or stationery letterhead. If you do decide to publicize your mission statement, 'try it on' for several days or weeks before you go to the printer. Read it to yourself every morning before work. Does it sound good? feel right? fit well? Can you live up to it? Will it keep you on target and motivate you? Will it serve your employees, partners, company, customers, stockholders, and clients? You might even ask others for their feedback.

Once you've crafted your 'perfect' mission statement, realize that it's not etched in stone. It can change and evolve as you grow in wisdom, knowledge, and insight.

Back from the Future

When you plan your day, be sure that the activities on your 'to-do' list relate to your mission statement. Then schedule time to work on those activities. This way, no matter how hectic a particular day has been, you've still accomplished something important, which gives you a sense of progress and keeps your energy high.

One way to determine if you're working on the right thing at any given time is to use the "Back from the Future" technique described by Peter Turla, president of the National Management Institute in the Dallas/Forth Worth area. He invites people to:

Pretend that it's a year from now—or five or ten years, or the end of your life—and you're looking back on today. Will you be able to say that you used your time wisely and that today was spent well?

With your mission statement in hand to guide and inspire you, you'll be able to answer "yes" to the questions above. You'll embrace work with greater enthusiasm, create more prosperity—economic, social, and spiritual—for yourself and others, and conduct business in a way that enriches yourself as well as those with whom you work.

An 11-Step Plan to Achieve Your Good

Now that you've drafted a mission statement for yourself, here's a plan to help you achieve your goals:

1. Put your clearly defined, long- and short-term goals in writing for your job, career, social life, finances, spiritual development, health, and other major areas. Just as your spoken word shapes your experiences, your written word focuses your mental energies. Putting your goals in writing encourages you to think logically, strengthens your commitment to your objectives, and encourages you to follow through. Keep your written goals in a daily planning book for quick reference and review.

2. To determine your priorities, ask yourself, "If I had only six months to live, what would I regret not having done? What would I want to have accomplished?" Asking questions like these can help you target what's really important to you.

3. Focus on the results you want, not on the process. Instead of making it a goal to clean your desk, for example, write, "I work at a clean, well-organized desk." After you write down each goal, take a few minutes to consider how it relates to your spiritual development.

4. Write each goal in positive terms. Instead of having as a goal "I'm going to stop being so pessimistic," have as a goal "I'm a happy, positive person who inspires others. I think of problems as opportunities to find creative solutions and I look forward to coming to work."

5. Break your goal into manageable steps with a completion date for each step. For example, "I want to increase sales by 25 percent over the last quarter. To accomplish this, I'll contact five new prospects a day for the next three weeks, telephone two former customers on the first of each month to keep in touch, attend a sales training seminar, and call my regular customers to thank them for their business." Then reflect on what having increased sales means to you in spiritual terms. It might indicate that you have an increased faith in the abundance in the universe.

6. Make your goals measurable, such as "I know I'm evolving spiritually because I can find at least three positive things about everyone I meet and every challenge I encounter."

7. Recognize the problems you create for yourself by not having achieved your goal. For example, "When I feel negative, people avoid me, I get irritated easily, and I don't think as clearly."

8. List all the benefits you'll enjoy when you achieve your goal. For example, "Now that I'm making my desired income, I'm going to be able to pay the mortage, I can afford some luxuries, and I can be more generous with others," or "When I'm positive and spiritually attuned, I get more done, make wiser decisions, and have more energy. As a result, people are more willing to cooperate with me."

9. Test the strength of your desires. After you've broken a goal into steps with deadlines and measurable outcomes, decide how much time you're willing to spend each day

toward achieving it. If you aren't willing to spend even a minimal amount of time, choose another goal.

10. Develop a support system. Build a library of inspirational books, join a master-mind group, listen to motivational tapes, keep in touch with friends, and attend seminars on how to manage your time and achieve your goals.

11. Use regular, positive affirmations for each area of your life. This gives your daily activities purpose and meaning. Continue to look for ways to mesh a spiritual perspective with everything you do.

Live Life according to What You Value

Be sure that your daily activities relate to your valued objectives. A year from now, for example, do you want to be more spiritually attuned? If you do, instead of watching television tonight, meditate, read an inspiring book, or attend a study group. If one of your objectives is to express yourself through writing, singing, dancing, or painting, be sure to write, sing, dance, or paint every day. Then, no matter how hectic your day has been, you'll have accomplished something toward your overall mission, and you'll enjoy a richer, fuller life.

■

"If you have built castles in the air, your work need not be lost; that is where they should be. Now put foundations under them."

Henry David Thoreau

■

"The kingdom of God is within you."

Jesus, Luke 17:21

■

". . . the great thing in this world is not so much where we stand as in what direction we are moving."

Oliver Wendell Holmes

■

"The time you enjoy wasting is not wasted time."

Bertrand Russell

■

"Only the organized can loaf with peace of mind."

Author Unknown

■

On immortality: "The average man does not know what to do with his life, yet wants another one which will last forver."

Anatole France

■

"Happiness is not having what you want, it's wanting what you have."

Author Unknown

■

Chapter 3

How to Gain Spiritual Insights at Work

THE THINGS that happen daily at the office can give you valuable insights into some of your deeper, unconscious belief systems. This can help you work with greater awareness, wisdom, and sensitivity.

The following six-step plan is the best way I've found to gain useful insights from business situations.

1. Select the Situation You Want to Interpret

Give one situation your full attention before trying to understand another. For the sake of this exercise, let's suppose that you were just fired from a job and you want to understand the experience more fully.

2. Affirm the *Real* 'Bottom Line'

There is a spiritual foundation to all experiences, even to difficult ones like being fired, and you can interpret an event in a way that will help you become a more complete, more aware human being.

3. Identify the Spiritual Influences in the Experience

Look for the following spiritual laws—operating either individually or in combination—that might be influencing a situation:

- Unity: There's a larger Reality—a universal Energy—behind
  and within all things visible and invisible; you were created
  from It and therefore are one with It.
- Cause and Effect: You have a say in creating your experiences. The circumstances in your life are often outward
  expressions of your beliefs.
- Attraction: Like attracts like. What you dwell on tends to
  appear in your experience.
- Circulation and Release: Energy is always in motion. You
  either interfere with this free flow of energy by being fearful or you encourage it by being positive and sharing your
  time, talent, energy, and resources.
- Resurrection: Energy is neither created nor destroyed, only
  transformed.

4. Think about the Symbols or Metaphors Involved in the Experience and Look for the Lessons

A metaphor is a figure of speech that compares two items by
stating that one item *is* the other: the sun (with its yellow rays)
is a lion or, conversely, a lion (with its yellow mane) is a sun.

Aristotle believed that the ability to think metaphorically was
the *single* characteristic of genius because it integrates diverse
disciplines, such as astronomy and zoology, as in the example
above, and integrates diverse types of intelligence, such as the
poetic and the scientific. Metaphoric thinking is a holistic approach to viewing the world, which resembles having an expan-
sive, spiritual perspective.

To apply this approach to business, think of an outward experience, event, or circumstance as an outpicturing of some in-

ternal thought process. This enables you to make meaningful, sometimes surprising, connections. It may also help you to see situations as depicting a greater truth—something higher, deeper, and more significant than the actual event itself. The lessons come from these realizations.

Thinking of a real fire as representing the *experience* of being fired, for example, encourages you to make associations. Fire in a forest destroys the old to make way for the new. Maybe being fired destroyed the tangled 'underbrush' in your life to make way for something better. Or maybe it's an invitation to get 'fired up' about doing the kind of work you really want to do instead of the work you had been doing.

It's also possible that certain events represent some need within yourself, at least in part. Maybe a part of you, for example, was ready to be purified, ready for the underbrush to be cleared away. And, with this end in mind, you might even have helped instigate things by tossing a 'match' on the 'pile.'

If something happens once, such as being fired, running out of gas on the way to work, or misplacing your keys, it might just indicate that you need to pay better attention to what you're doing. If you often run out of gas or usually misplace things, it could represent a belief system that you have, which could use some looking at. With that in mind, what *might* the following events represent?

Event	Possible Belief System, Need, or Desire
• Running out of gas on the way to work	Low energy regarding your job, a wish to be headed in another direction; resisting commitment; feeling trapped or obligated.
• Having good credit	Generous with the credit you give others; deserving of the credit you've earned; a belief in abundance and prosperity.

- Having bad credit or going over your credit limit

  Withholding praise or acknowledgment from others; not receiving all the credit you're due; taking credit for other people's ideas or work; a belief in limitation.

- Bouncing a check or forgetting to pay a bill

  Withholding something from others: money, love, praise, acknowledgment; a need to hold on to your money as long as possible, a belief in scarcity.

- Getting a raise, promotion, award, or an important contract

  On the right track, high profile, keeping up the good work; healthy self-esteem; a belief in yourself.

- Misplacing items: keys, an assignment, an important document, your umbrella, etc.

  Misplacing the key to (or the understanding of) something, losing sight of priorities, looking for shelter or security.

5. Give Thanks for What You Already Have

When you really think about it, you have more that goes right in your life than goes wrong. You have family, friends, abilities, food, shelter, and probably an academic education or an education gained through life experiences. Remembering this puts you in a more positive frame of mind, which in turn increases your receptivity to more good.

6. Look to the Future

It's the nature of Life to evolve, change, and make progress. Since you are one with Life, it's also *your* nature to evolve, change, and make progress. To do this, you must let go of any resentment, anger, or guilt that might be holding you back. You must move forward, secure in knowing that Infinite Intelligence responds to your needs and creates what you desire.

Now let's look at some ways that people have applied these ideas.

Like Attracts Like

The CEO of a consulting firm wanted to enlarge his client base. He decided to explore the Law of Attraction and work consciously with it.

First he acknowledged the importance of advertising to a business. He knew that, usually, the clearer the ad, the more effective it is. Then he contemplated avertising itself as a symbol. He had the insight that advertising takes on universal dimensions when we realize that we attract experiences for which we 'advertise' on an unconscious level. The 'customers' who answer our ads are particular events, experiences, and people.

He began to notice that what he actively and regularly thought about manifested and multiplied. He concluded that if he became more positive, he would tend to attract more clients. So he enlarged his spiritual advertising budget. His 'ad campaign' included meditating regularly, reading inspirational material, listening to motivational tapes on his way to work, attending classes, associating with enthusiastic, like-minded people, and giving thanks for the clients he already had.

As a result of his winning 'advertising campaign,' there was a corresponding positive shift in his success. Previous clients gave him repeat business and recommended him to others. In the following months his business doubled, and it has been growing steadily ever since.

If you're an employee instead of an employer, you can have a similar advertising campaign. In addition to attracting positive people into your experience, you might also attract a bonus, special recognition, or promotion.

You Are One with the
Source of Infinite Abundance

Several years ago I had an excellent opportunity to learn about Infinite Abundance when a promoter who generated 90 percent of my company's seminar business went bankrupt. He'd been doing so well for so long that I'd come to rely on him as my only source of income. When he went bankrupt he owed my company a great deal of money. In addition, our volume of business dropped significantly.

Instead of going into a panic I looked beyond the seemingly grim circumstances and affirmed that all of us who were affected by the bankruptcy were enterprising individuals with a surplus of ideas and creative energy. Because people are spiritual in nature I knew that prosperity is our birthright. I claimed my right to be rich in all things: wisdom, health, friends, creative ideas, and money. And I gave thanks for all the good I already had. Then I looked to the future instead of using my valuable energy to dwell on my former promoter's temporary misfortune, or on mine.

In time he used the bankruptcy experience to regroup, heal himself, and begin again. Today he's involved in new and lucrative projects.

As for myself, I saw the lull in business activity as an opportunity to explore new marketing strategies, to diversify, and to write the highly successful audio-cassette program *How to Organize Yourself to Win*, which became a phenomenal best-seller.

Your Experiences Exist to Promote
Your Personal Growth

A writer who was plagiarized twice by a co-worker had this to say about how she used spiritual principles to deal with the situation and learn from it: "I had a long talk with the man who claimed that he hadn't known he was doing anything wrong when he copied entire pages of my published, copyrighted book and got them published and copyrighted under his own name.

"After weeks of wrestling with my anger I concluded that I'd only hurt my own creativity if I dwelled on what happened. I didn't need revenge. The universe, through the Law of Cause and Effect, would hold him responsible for his actions, most likely in ways unknown to me.

"Turning the problem over to a Higher Authority gave me the freedom to move on. I drew up a contract for the man to sign that clearly protected my work, then daily affirmed that I had creative, ethical people in my life. He signed the contract and, a few weeks later, went to work for another company.

"In retrospect I realize that it was as if the two of us were standing by a great reservoir of Infinite Creativity and I was fiercely protecting a cup of 'water' that I had drawn. He wanted the 'water' that I had. When I resented him, I forgot that I could get more water. And he didn't know he could get his own.

"I also realized that, ultimately, my Higher Self is the co-author of my best work. I may not give Spirit a by-line on my articles, but now before I write, I get into a meditative state and acknowledge a working relationship with the source of Infinite Creativity.

"Since having these insights, and realizing that even difficult experiences can support my personal growth, I became more creative than ever, and in one year my income increased 10 times."

All Roads Lead to Your Greater Good

A successful entrepreneur shared this story about the time he got in with the 'wrong' crowd:

"I joined a company that I later discovered was run by an out-law, a rogue who was unethical and dishonest. I wondered how

I could have made such a 'bad' decision to work for that particular company. Through the experience, though, I made valuable contacts and gained a crucial knowledge of the industry. Eventually I found my way to a reputable company and finally started my own business, which is now growing rapidly.

"I concluded that if I'm standing at a fork in the road I can't take the 'wrong' road because God is in both forks. Ultimately there are no 'wrong' decisions. What at first seemed like a bad business decision served to point me in a better direction."

Difficulties Can Be Blessings in Disguise

Once one of my suppliers neglected to inform me that he was weeks behind in meeting the deadline for one of my company's products. Back orders were piling up, anxious customers were calling, and no one knew when he'd complete the job. Furthermore, he wouldn't return any of my telephone calls.

This was just one more difficulty in a long line of problems that I'd had with him. At first I was tempted to judge him, but then I realized that my condemnation wouldn't make him get the product out faster. If anything it might make him feel guilty or angry, which could affect the quality of his work. I also knew that the energy I would have spent judging him needed to be used more constructively.

I explained to my customers why their orders were late and apologized. Then I asked for bids from other suppliers and found one who came highly recommended who would charge less for filling the orders faster.

I had several insights from the crisis. First, I found another supplier who could easily meet the increasing demands for my future orders. By hiring someone else I released my first supplier to become successful at his own pace. He'd been under a great deal of pressure and might have needed to relax and to 'grow' his company more slowly.

Second, I realized that ultimately there are no crises in supply when we work with *universal* supply. There is only Infinite Abundance waiting for us to use it.

Third, I reaffirmed for myself that difficulties are blessings in disguise that point us in the right direction to receive something that's more appropriate, convenient, or beneficial for us. With these insights, I renewed my commitment to using spiritual principles in the workplace.

"The Broader the Base, the Higher the Tower"

The Universe is built on a foundation for good. How do I know? Because wouldn't it be awful if it weren't true?

As human beings we may never know, while we're in these bodies, exactly how Life operates at the deepest level. We may be limited in our complete understanding of a Higher/Inner Power, but we can believe the best of that Power. We can honor It by seeking It out, working with It consciously, and learning from our experiences. To have experiences and not to attempt to understand them is to litter spiritually.

When you act on your faith that there's a Power for good in the universe that responds to you, notice the results you get. If your present belief system isn't working for you in business, change that belief for a few months and see what happens. You can always go back to the old way if you want to.

Make a Spiritual Response Your First Response

Start today to look for spiritual significance in your job or business. If you encounter challenging situations, apply the six-step plan detailed in this chapter to gain insights. Make a spiritual response your first response, not your last resort. You'll find that you're becoming calmer, more centered, and less affected by temporary, difficult circumstances. You'll think more clearly and make better decisions. You'll have more energy and enthusiasm, and you'll attract positive, receptive people. You'll realize that a Higher Power is active in all your business affairs, and with this Power available to you, you can enjoy unlimited success.

"Human beings, by changing the inner attitudes of their minds, can change the outer aspects of their lives."

William James

"Be not afraid of growing slowly; be afraid only of standing still."

Chinese proverb

"When you are identified with the One, all things will be complete to you."

Chuang Tzu, The Record

"The whole contains nothing that is not for its advantage. By remembering that I am part of such a whole, I shall be content with everything that happens."

Marcus Aurelius, Meditations

"Astonishing! Everything is intelligent!"

Pythagoras

"There is a Power for good in the universe and you can use it."

Ernest Holmes

Chapter 4

The New Frontier

A PERSON can't practice spirituality in business," a CEO once told me. He explained that spirituality is an exclusive, personal relationship between an individual and that individual's concept of God Energy or a Higher Power. He said that spirituality is a subjective experience that cannot be quantified, qualified, manifested on the material plane, or easily discussed.

"The closest you can come to expressing your spirituality at work is by tuning in to your intuition when you make decisions," he concluded.

I agree that an individual's spirituality is highly personal, but as with all the great, universal concepts such as freedom, beauty, and love, we can demonstrate our understanding of the greater concept by expressing its qualities through our everyday actions.

Freedom, for example, means "liberty from slavery, oppression, or incarceration," or "the condition of being free from constraints." Two ways that we can manifest our understanding of this universal concept is to vote and to take an active stand against oppression when we see it happening.

Another concept—beauty—means "a pleasing quality associated with harmony of form or color." We each relate to beauty, however, in our own personal ways. Some of us, for example, show an understanding of beauty by landscaping our lawns or decorating our homes. Others of us dress in style, appreciate a sunset, paint a picture, hike in the mountains, or stop to smell the flowers.

Love, also considered a universal concept, is "an intense affection for another person." When people are in love, however, they do certain things to express that love such as spending time together, giving each other tokens of that love, looking forward to spending more time together, and exploring ways to deepen their relationship.

Likewise when people have a working relationship with a Greater Power, they find themselves naturally expressing this relationship in their lives.

At the office, for example, we can demonstrate our personal relationship with, to quote Ernest Holmes, the "Unity behind all things," by having integrity, ethics, compassion for others, and respect for the planet. By doing so, we re-enact our divine nature in the workplace.

Life-Affirming Alternatives

Look in any bookstore and you'll find evidence that people are demonstrating a greater concern for global issues and seeing themselves and their companies in relation to the Whole. They are opting for more life-affirming alternatives to the popular 'warfare' model of business, with all its bravado and frantic scrambling to seize the largest market share. Growing numbers of executives across the country are:

- showing greater respect for their employees by inviting and rewarding creative, individual contributions to the company
- fostering teamwork and morale
- encouraging and acknowledging individual accomplishments and providing for career enhancement

- choosing to cooperate instead of compete, both within the company and between companies
- embracing diversity
- exploring ways to incorporate values, ethics, and integrity into the workplace to make work a more enjoyable, rewarding experience for all involved

There's no limit to corporate creativity when an organization decides to express spiritual principles in business. Here are some of the things that people are doing:

- A publishing company in New York provides a meditation room on the premises and allows time for employees to use it if they wish.
- The president of a successful advertising agency in California regularly practices yoga, meditates, and reads inspirational material, which increases his sense of well-being and his ability to make wise decisions.
- A talent agency in southern California sends models and actors only to those assignments whose products reflect life-enhancing values.
- Companies are realizing the importance of humor, and some have appointed 'negativity patrols,' 'ambassadors of fun,' 'morale czars' or 'lieutenants of laughs' to help to keep people's spirits high.
- More companies are donating a percentage of their profits to worthy causes.
- Corporations are becoming more conscious of their effects on the global economy and on the environment.

And growing numbers of employees are responding in kind by:

- working with renewed interest and dedication
- buying stock in the company

- looking for creative solutions to challenges that face the organization
- taking advantage of training and development opportunities offered by the company so they can be more productive as employees on the job
- recycling office products
- joining with management to meet the company's goals
- looking for ways to cooperate with others as part of a team
- exploring ways they can enjoy greater job satisfaction and consequently be more valuble to the company

People report that this positive approach is paying off in a big way. They're enjoying increased personal fulfillment, greater job satisfaction, and more profit. They're finding that when they put people and quality products before profit, the business naturally thrives.

32 Ideas for Developing a Socially Conscious Workplace

To develop a more socially responsible way of doing business that fosters a higher regard for people and a greater respect for the planet, consider the following ideas:

Conserve Energy

1. Conduct energy audits of the office building and, where energy is being wasted, find ways to conserve it.
2. Carpool and telecommute.
3. Schedule conference calls rather than ask people to travel to attend meetings.
4. Use outside air in the winter for cooling, if possible, and the sun for heat in the summers.

Protect the Environment

5. Assess the company's impact on the environment and find ways to solve problems.
6. Support environmental programs in the community.
7. Use popcorn packing material instead of Styrofoam 'peanuts.'
8. Keep the costs of products low by keeping overhead low.
9. Use alternatives to animal testing and animal by-products.
10. Treat waste products effectively.
11. Recycle paper products and chemicals.
12. Use soybean inks.
13. Shred paper and use as packing material.
14. Make double-sided copies when possible.
15. Use refillable pens and reusable dishes.
16. Recycle phone books and printer cartridges.
17. Compost biodegradable products.

Education and Community Outreach Programs

18. Invest in the training of staff, customers, and the community.
19. Educate while you advertise.
20. Provide grants, scholarships, and apprenticeship programs.
21. Give people time off to participate in yearly Earth Day celebrations.
22. Sponsor community programs, mulching events, and seminars.
23. Participate in food collections.
24. Support ethnic business.
25. Donate a percentage of your profits to nonprofit causes.

Social

26. Offer—or attend—workshops on diversity.
27. Promote literacy.
28. Support programs for the arts.
29. Provide day care for employees' children.
30. Involve employees in formulating policy and standard practices.
31. Reward innovative thinking.
32. Do business with companies that donate a percentage of profits to worthy social causes.

When you have a working relationship with a greater Power, you'll find yourself naturally expressing this relationship in your life. And the workplace will become an extension of your values, with all the attendant characteristics: integrity, ethics, and compassion.

The CEO mentioned in the beginning of this chapter, incidentally, had a change of mind/heart and became the founder of a company that publishes books that encourage and support the evolution of consciousness in the business community.

■

"God enters by a private door into every individual."
Ralph Waldo Emerson

■

"You are what you love."

St. Augustine

■

"For the body is one and has many members, but all the members of that one body, being many, are one body."

Paul, 1 Corinthians 12:12

■

"You know Me in you, and from this knowledge you will derive all that is necessary."
St. Catherine of Siena, Dialogue

■

"The world is missing what can be found in you."
James Miller

■

Chapter 5

How to Align Your Business Goals with Your Values

MAYBE YOU'VE seen them—businesspeople who are so intent upon achieving their long-term goals that they don't seem to enjoy each day.

They're like the people who hop into their cars and race to get somewhere so they can begin to enjoy themselves once they arrive. They're so preoccupied with reaching a destination that they rarely stop for breaks, they risk getting speeding tickets or becoming stressed out, and they ignore the sights. They fail to realize that getting somewhere can be fun, too, and that there is a way to arrive at a destination feeling relaxed and good about themselves.

Maybe you know people like this. Maybe *you* are one. If you are, it might be helpful to examine the difference between goals and values.

The Difference between Goals and Values

The destination, the objective, represents a goal. The quality of the trip, the style with which you do a particular activity, reflects your values. Goals are measurable because they have beginnings and, usually, endings. Values are the underlying principles behind your goals. Values, which are infinite, give your life quality, depth, and significance.

What Do You Value?

A long-term goal in your job or business might be to get promoted, get rich, or become famous. A short-term goal might be to make enough money to pay the rent or the mortgage, do a good job on a current project, or meet an upcoming deadline.

The style with which you achieve these business objectives determines the quality of your daily life. With this in mind, I invite you to explore your values as they relate to your professional life.

1. List your values. If you're interested in professional growth, your list might include being honest, having integrity, and expressing your creativity.
2. Ask yourself how strongly you feel about each of your listed values. Are they simply qualities that it would be nice to develop, or are they qualities on which you're willing to work every day?
3. Decide which values to strengthen and deepen as they relate to your goals.

    • If one of your goals is to raise funds or increase your earning potential, and you value integrity, for example, you can strive to make money honestly. You can practice truth in advertising when you promote your product or your service. And you can be honest with yourself and others.
    • If one of your goals is to make wise business decisions, and you value intelligence and wisdom, you can affirm

that Spirit within you knows the answers and makes the right decisions for the good of all involved. It's easier to make the right decision when you make the choices that move you closer to your clearly defined values.

- If one of your goals is to increase your client or customer base, and you value compassion or understanding, you can express those values through the service that you give to others. You can be compassionate with people who are being difficult, and helpful and caring with customers and clients.

When you relate what you do at work to your overall values, you'll tend to have more energy, feel a greater sense of purpose, and be more enthusiastic. Work becomes more meaningful when you use it to express your highest values.

Little Changes, Great Results

Little changes over a period of time can produce great results. It's like giving up eating a daily pat of butter to achieve your ideal weight. One pat of butter a day may not seem like much, but over a year you've eaten a lot less butter, which can add up to a significant weight loss.

You may know people who are more successful in business than most, but they don't seem to work any harder. What do they do? Little things, every day, that add up to success. You can do this, too.

If you value being compassionate, for example, you don't have to try to be a Mother Teresa. You can affirm your oneness with all Life and daily strive to be more understanding and patient with the people with whom you come in contact. And every day, in little ways, you become a more caring human being.

If you value intelligence, you don't have to try to be an Albert Einstein or a Stephen Hawking. We're *all* geniuses. The trick is to express your genius more often more consistently. You can begin to do this by realizing that Divine Intelligence operates through you and that when you calm your outer mind and allow yourself to be guided by an Inner Knowing, the answers come. Every day you make wiser, more intelligent choices and decisions. In time it all adds up, and you find yourself enjoying greater success.

How to Enhance Your Business Goals

To upgrade the style with which you achieve your job or career objectives, consider having a daily value on which to work, such as tolerance, patience, creativity, compassion, or understanding. Then look for opportunities to express that value. To keep it in mind:

- Write it on a 3-by-5 card on your desk.
- Write it at the top of your daily to-do list.
- Use it as your personal password, if you need one, to access your computer programs or go online.

And now, instead of getting mired in details and routines, you'll see your job responsibilities, no matter how seemingly insignificant, as opportunities to practice your values.

At the end of each day, reflect on how well you expressed that day's particular value. If you need more practice, work on the same value the next day. If you did well, congratulate yourself on the progress you made and move on to another value. If you encountered a difficult situation, consider how you might have handled it from a spiritual perspective and reflect on what you learned from it. Then ask yourself, "Did I work today according to what I value?"

What's Your Scenario?

If someone followed you around the office all day and recorded your activities, then tried to construct a scenario of what you value, would that person have an accurate picture?

Perhaps an observer would conclude from your actions that one of your great ambitions is to shuffle papers, encourage interruptions, stretch your coffee breaks, or procrastinate.

Might it be better, instead, to align your goals with your values and have people conclude that you care about professional growth, teamwork, satisfied customers, and doing the best job that you can?

'Having Done' versus 'Doing'

A highly successful author, with more than 83 books published, confided to me that he wasn't totally happy being a writer. He admitted, "I don't like to write; I like having written."

This is unfortunate, because in life 'having done' is behind us. 'Doing,' however, is ongoing and takes most of our time. So let's savor each moment along the way to achieving our goals. Let's let our most cherished values enrich our goals and give meaning to our jobs and our careers. Let's do our work with style and confidence. And most of all, let's enjoy the trip.

■

"The whole Universe is on your side. Life is forever biased on the side of healing, on the side of overcoming, on the side of success. When you get yourself centered in the Universal flow, you become synchronized with this divine bias for good."

Eric Butterworth,
Spiritual Economics: The Prosperity Process

■

"May you live all the days of your life."

Jonathan Swift

■

"The Universe is a friendly place."

Albert Einstein

■

"You are today where your thoughts have brought you; you will be tomorrow where your thoughts take you."

James Allen

■

Chapter 6

The Get-by Job

HAVE YOU ever found yourself in employment that didn't seem to be the best place for you? That happened to me many years ago when I was doing office work in a detoxification center for alcoholics—a far cry from being able to use my teaching credential or my degrees in reading education and creative writing.

At first I found the job interesting because of the people with whom I associated. The staff was caring and dedicated, and the people who came through the program had a variety of fascinating stories to share. But the weeks grew into months, and the months into years. I continued to write thank-you letters for donations, type proposals, write thank-you letters, duplicate everything and mail the originals and file the copies.

One day I looked up from my desk and realized that I'd been working there for three years. I felt trapped. My dissatisfaction turned into desperation. I wasn't making the money I wanted, I had no chance of a promotion, and I wasn't using my talents. I loved to write and teach, but finding employment in those professions seemed hopeless. I didn't have any plans. I had stopped writing and had given up looking for teaching opportunities. I was in the proverbial rut.

The Real Cause of Job Dissatisfaction

My spiritual philosophy sustained me through the discouraging times. I finally concluded that I was frustrated more because of my beliefs about prosperity and employment than by the job itself. I had to deal with my dissatisfaction on that level rather than complain about the effect of those beliefs—my job. If I didn't examine those underlying attitudes, I might always have 'get-by' jobs. I wanted to understand *why* I was in that situation before I decided *what* to do about it. I vowed to stay in that job until I understood myself in relation to it. Then I'd be free to move on.

If you're in a similar situation, you might want to consider some of the following ideas.

Your Job as Symbol

Think of your job as an outpicturing of some belief that you might have. For me, I wondered how I'd come to work in a detoxification center when I wasn't addicted to anything. As I examined my beliefs about teaching and writing, for which I was truly suited, I realized that I *was* addicted—to the belief that teachers couldn't find jobs and that writers starved. And sure enough, that was what was happening in my life.

Day after discouraging day in the detoxification center I saw creative, gifted people trading their talents, even their very lives, for their addictions. Some would be sober for months, then 'lose it,' returning to their fears and beliefs in limitations. In a sense, I had been no different.

Know Who You Really Are

You are much more than just your job, where you live, your social status, or even your name. You are the full expression of the universe, animated by Life. You therefore have tremendous power to determine your experiences and create prosperity for yourself.

The more I realized this union with Life, the more I admitted that I'd had greater control than I'd previously thought when it came to creating my experiences. When I'd accepted the position in the detoxification center, I knew what the salary was and exactly what duties were expected of me. Yet there I was, blaming the job for my not being challenged and for my lack of prosperity. The job wasn't responsible, nor were my employers—*I* was!

I had seen my job as my only source of income and, in doing so, had closed down the possibilities of getting employment that really suited me. Since I'd made the decision to stay in that particular job for a while, I had to stop wasting my valuable energy complaining and put it to good use thinking of new ways to prosper.

A Personal Detoxification Program

If you feel stuck in a get-by job, take some time every day to write down creative ways that you could make additional money. Welcome every idea no matter how impractical some of them might seem. After you've made your list, pick the ideas on which you'd be willing to work in your spare time, then jot down an action plan for achieving those goals.

Study people who are successful doing work they love to do, and use them as role models. In my case I remembered that I knew two people who were living very comfortably off the income (advances and royalties) from their poetry and novels. Funny how I'd forgotten about them when I was in the throes of dissatisfaction.

I also knew a number of people who were teaching classes in corporations—a possibility I hadn't considered. I started to attend their combination social/business meetings and I relaxed my picture of what a teaching job would look like. Teaching can take many forms. I didn't need to work every day in a public school. I could be a private tutor, work in a private school, be a visiting teacher for students who had to miss school for some reason, or work with adults in business and industry.

I finally convinced myself that teachers could find work and that writers could survive very well. And I was determined to be one of them!

Prepare for Success

They say that luck favors the well prepared. With this in mind, talk to people in your desired profession or area of interest, make contacts, network, do some reading, maybe take a class or two to update your skills. In my case, I brushed off a reading course that I'd been teaching off and on, redesigned the workbook and the visuals, and updated the information. I enjoyed teaching the course but didn't like to market it, so I didn't teach it very often. I figured that maybe when the course was ready, a promoter would appear.

"Thank You"

Then one day as I mailed off what must have been my two-thousandth thank-you letter at the detoxification center, it occurred to me that maybe *I* wasn't saying "thank you" enough. I'd been focusing on what I didn't have rather than on what I did have: supportive friends, health, a dependable income, and two cheerful, accommodating bosses who let me adjust my schedule when I needed time off.

I bought a supply of postcards and started to thank people for their good service, for their friendship, and even for how nicely they kept their yards. The more I thanked people, the happier I felt. And amazing things started to happen. I met a man who offered a series of one-day programs to businesspeople throughout the country. I sent him a proposal for my reading-skills course, he hired me, and my class was included in a catalogue that was mailed out annually to several million people.

On the Road Again

So I quit my get-by job and have been traveling all over the country ever since, teaching my course, visiting friends and family along the way, and making 10–15 times the salary I was making at my old job. My income varies because the number of clients varies that I have each year.

I got to arrange my schedule, so I had three to four weeks off at a stretch during which time I did nothing but write. I was a columnist for *Success* magazine for five years, had three books published, and wrote and produced a best-selling audio-cassette tape album.

Why did I need almost four years working in a detoxification center to learn my lessons about prosperity and employment? Couldn't I have learned them faster? Obviously not. Actually, four years is a short time to have undone the belief in limitation that I'd been entertaining and nurturing all my life. Besides, if I'd left the detoxification center any sooner, my ideal job wouldn't have been ready for me. The man who founded the business that so successfully promoted me and 28 other speakers was still working in *his* get-by job and preparing to start his own seminar business. That job eventually evolved into a private consulting business for myself and, as of this writing, I've just been scheduled to teach 36 classes in one year for one company alone. And I'm writing another book.

It turns out that my get-by job hadn't been an accidental detour in my life, but rather a necessary step along the way toward my greater fulfillment as a human being. You too may discover that when you examine your beliefs about employment and prosperity in relation to your work, you're always in the right employment for your spiritual growth—no matter what the job.

■

"Think of your career as your ministry. Make your work an expression of love in service to mankind."
Marianne Williamson, A Return to Love

■

"Anyone who has a *why* to live can bear almost any *what*."

Nietzsche

■

"Nothing is either good or bad. It's thinking that makes it so."

William Shakespeare

■

"Cherish your visions; cherish your ideals; cherish the music that stirs in your heart, the beauty that forms in your mind, the loveliness that drapes your purest thoughts, for . . . if you remain true to them, your world will at last be built."

James Allen

■

Chapter 7

My Job/Myself?

DO YOU treat your job as though work is separate from yourself, just something that you do from nine to five on weekdays only and turn off at the end of the day? The way you approach your job, however, may reflect the way you approach life in general. Understanding this could provide you with valuable insights into some of your more basic beliefs. Here are nine creative ways to think about your job.

1. You Are Greater than Your Job

As a spiritual being you are greater than any experience or circumstance. You have emotions, for example; but more importantly, you have an infinite spirit that far exceeds and outlives temporary emotions or events. You have a house, but you also live on a spiritual plane. You have a body, but it's just on loan. And if you have a job, it's a projection, in part, of your beliefs. You have a say in making it what it is—and what it isn't.

Spirit responds to your creative thoughts and manifests them for you. Your job—or lack of a job—is the way that you choose to express your attitudes about prosperity and employment.

2. What Does Your Job Symbolize?

First consider the objective definition of your job. For example: an author is one who originates or creates in words; a construction worker builds, assembles, or tears down; a financial consultant advises people on money matters; a lawyer interprets and defends the law; and a teacher instructs.

Then consider the subjective meaning of your job, what it personally symbolizes for you. If you're an author, for example, you might examine how you're 'writing' the story of your life. You also might have fun figuring out what genre of writing—romance, science fiction, thriller, melodrama, poetry, or mystery —most closely resembles your life, or parts of it.

If you're a construction worker, you might look at how you construct your partnerships, relationships, or finances—and in what ways, if any, you tear them down. Also consider the kinds of buildings you construct, such as shopping malls, prisons, amusement parks, or single-family dwellings, and how those structures might mirror something that you're thinking or feeling at this particular time in your life.

If you're a financial consultant, you might figure out how well you're managing your own finances. You also might look at the business issues or relationships in which you invest your time, money, or beliefs. Are you getting high returns on those investments?

If you're a lawyer, you might analyze the symbol of law and judgment in your life. Are you a prosecutor, a defense attorney, or a corporate lawyer? Do you prosecute or defend people in general, or are *you* prosecuted or defended in some way, in some particular area, by others? Are you in tune with spiritual law?

If you're a teacher or child-care worker, might there be an inner child who needs your love and attention?

Realize that whatever your job, you are unfolding and evolving spiritually through it. You can expect the best.

3. Consider the Opposite

After you've looked at the objective and subjective meanings of your job, consider the opposite implications. If you're a teacher, for example, is there something that you need to learn for a change? If you're a health-care worker, instead of always taking care of others, are there issues in your own life that you need to heal?

I knew a public-health inspector who went for months without cleaning her own home, a landfill consultant who was a 'pack rat,' a memory expert who often misplaced things, and a receptionist who was gracious with customers but extremely strict with her own children, and unreceptive to their ideas.

Each of these people had an opportunity to use their jobs to learn more about themselves and to examine how their work reflected areas of their lives where they needed more harmony and balance.

4. Freed from Limitations

When I finally detoxified myself from my 'addiction' to a belief in limitations, discussed in the previous chapter, and found employment as a writer and a teacher, my assignments often reflected some inner process with which I was dealing. I began my career by writing a column for *Success* magazine. Why did I write for that magazine instead of *Good Housekeeping*, *Cat Fancy*, or *People* magazine? Maybe because I was dealing with personal issues of success at that time. After all, I had just come out of 'detox.'

Likewise, the clients who took my management trainings reflected inner issues on which I was working. At various times I worked with bankers (personal issues of finance and investing), missionaries (issues about manifesting my spiritual beliefs in my outer experience), and heart specialists (issues about being more expressive on a feeling level).

Realize how each of your job assignments allows you to look at some challenging area of your life and transform your beliefs for the better.

5. What Do Your Responsibilities Symbolize?

After you examine what your job symbolizes in general, look at what your particular responsibilities signify.

- Do you purchase supplies? Could there be an order you need to place in Spirit for something you want?
- Do you write meeting agendas? Is there a spiritual or an emotional agenda of your own that you need to clarify?
- Are you an accountant? Do you realize what really counts in your life, what's truly important?
- Are you a real estate agent? What do you sell? Commercial property, repossessed buildings, mansions, starter homes, 'fixer-uppers'? Might this say something about your aspirations, needs, or spiritual outlook at this time?

Realize that Life (God, Inner Management) inspires you, if you're receptive, to make the right decisions and choices. Each job assignment allows you to look at some challenging area of your life and to transform your beliefs for your greater good.

6. Why Do You Work?

Do you work for love or money—or both? Do you work to share your talents, express your creativity, or learn something? Are you working at a 'get-by' job until your 'real' job comes along? What do these things say about your motivation, ambition, goal-setting skills, outlook, or perseverance?

Do you make a minimum wage or a hefty salary? Do you think you're worth what you make? If you make less than you feel you should, are you looking for opportunities to advance yourself or looking for ways to increase your income?

Realize that a paycheck is only one way that you can make money and only one way that you can feel fulfilled by your work. Life is really the source of your supply and fulfillment.

7. My Job/My Parents?

A young man once told me, "I'm doing what my parents told me to do. They'd pay my college tuition only if I went into the career that they chose for me. So maybe my job says more about my parents than about me."

Not really. If you're working in a job or a career that someone else chose for you, the job probably still symbolizes something that you need to learn. It might reflect a need for you to be more assertive or it might reveal a family dynamic that needs to be healed.

Someone else may have told you to do that kind of work—but you went along with it. You went on the interview, agreed to those wages, and signed the contract—and it's *you* who show up every day.

When you consider your job from a spiritual perspective, things tend to fall into place, obstacles fall away, and the whole universe supports your making good money doing work that you love.

8. Where Do You Work?

Does your job location reveal anything about the current condition of your life: the way you do things, your inner strengths, or things about yourself that you want to improve?

- **Hospital emergency room.** Does your life outside the hospital tend to be full of emergencies? You might want to take some time to listen to your intuition. It can give you insights into how you may be helping create some of the crises in your life. It can also give you ideas on how to avert subsequent disasters. You additionally might want to look for less stressful ways to fill your need for excitement. On the other hand, maybe working in an emergency ward reflects an inner strength that you have. You might be good at helping people who are in physical or emotional pain. If you want to grow personally and spiritually, you might consider exploring ways to be of greater service to people wherever you meet them.

- **Offshore drilling rig.** Do you leave the mainland—what's conventional, established, and ordinary—to go to work? Do you tend to prefer a less traditional way of doing things? Does this style of working and living support your spiritual growth?

- **Convenience store.** Are things too easy—too convenient—for you? Have you become complacent regarding your spiritual growth? You might consider stretching your thinking. Join a study group, read a book on comparative religions, or attend a conference to meet new people, network, and exchange ideas. On the other hand, maybe your life has become too complicated. If this is the case, you might look at ways to simplify it.

- **Radio station.** Do you work in a place that broadcasts ideas to a wide listening audience? If you work at a radio station —or in a TV studio or at a newspaper—it could be an invitation for you to think about how effectively you fulfill your need to reach out to people.

- **Toll booth.** Do you work in the confined environment of a tool booth? The world passes you by, and yet, everyone gives you money. You might want to become more aware of the continuous flow of opportunities that life presents you.

- **Home.** Do you work at home? Are you doing your spiritual homework too?

No matter where you work, you can use your job to gain insights into yourself, your behavior, and your beliefs. And in doing so, you may find a renewed appreciation for the work you do.

9. An Opportunity for Personal Growth

Some of us choose particular jobs for the opportunity to master our fears or to stretch ourselves intellectually, physically, or spiritually. And in doing so, our greatest 'weaknesses' can become our greatest strengths.

I know several dynamic professional speakers who have stage fright, but who give enthusiastic, inspiring presentations in spite of it; numerous salespeople who are afraid of being 'rejected,' but who've become top salespeople in their fields; and counselors who've overcome their own emotional problems to become excellent therapists.

When you acknowledge your feelings about work and determine what motivates and inspires you, you'll survive the challenges with greater creativity and humor. You'll work more consciously, make wiser choices, and be more open to divine guidance.

On Track

When people talk to me about my spirituality-in-business books and articles, I often ask them what they do for a living. I consider their answers to be invitations for me to examine some aspect of my own life. When I asked one person what he did, he said, "I'm a track inspector for the railroad."

So here's one for you. Are you 'on track' in business or with your career? Might it be time to inspect the track you're on, switch tracks, or repair your track? If you're using spiritual principles on the job, pat yourself on the back—you are on the right track!

■

"It's important to run not on the fast track, but on your track. Pretend that you have only six months to live, and make three lists: the things you have to do, want to do, and neither have to do nor want to do. Then, for the rest of your life, forget everything on the third list."

Robert Eliot, Professor of Cardiology,
University of Nebraska

■

"Only those who develop their minds and spirits to the utmost can serve Heaven and fulfill their own destinies."

Mencius

■

"We are what we repeatedly do. Excellence, then, is not an act, but a habit."

Aristotle

■

"To be spiritual means seeking wisdom from the essence of things, not from their surface or appearance."

John McMurphy, Secrets from Great Minds

■

"I exist as I am—that is enough. If no other in the world be aware, I sit content. And if each and all be aware, I sit content."

Walt Whitman, Leaves of Grass

■

Chapter 8

What to Do When It's Been One of *Those* Days

WE KNOW that life is a learning experience. Have you ever had a day, though, when you wished that you could have stayed home from school? You know the kind of day I'm talking about. One of those days when nothing seems to go right.

Maybe there was a tie-up in traffic, you arrived late to the office, got behind in your work, and spent your lunch hour trying to catch up. Maybe a supplier neglected to inform you that he couldn't meet your deadline and impatient customers occupied most of your afternoon with demands. Then it was time for the weekly staff meeting, which dragged on and on. At quitting time, your 'to-do' list was your 'didn't-get-done' list.

How can you salvage a hectic day like this? Here are nine ideas.

1. Rise above Murphy's Law

Difficult days occasionally happen to even the most positive of us. Keeping a spiritual perspective, however, will prevent a 'bad' day from gathering momentum and turning into an even more difficult week.

Once I discontinued doing business with one of my manufacturers. When I asked him for my artwork and the masters of the tapes that he used for my project, he replied that he couldn't find any of the originals. His assistant shrugged and said, "Murphy's Law." She was referring to the belief that some people have, that "If something can go wrong, it will."

This had the makings of a major disaster for me, with the fate of a million-dollar account hanging in the balance.

Fortunately I don't subscribe to Murphy's Law. I subscribe instead to Universal Law, which, simply put, states that we create our own experiences with our beliefs. If, on a metaphysical level, I somehow created this problem for myself, I also had the power to solve the problem.

I affirmed that no matter how difficult circumstances appear to be, the truth is that there is a Higher Power within us and at the core of every situation. And, because we are one with this Universal Mind, we are empowered with infinite creativity and intelligence. Any problem, therefore, can be solved. This knowledge calmed and inspired me through the following days.

For three days the manufacturer's staff looked for the originals, then gave up. Still, I had faith that a Higher Power was working in this situation and through all the people involved. I had total confidence that this problem would be solved, although I had no idea how or when.

Because I knew there had to be a solution, I insisted that the manufacturer continue to look—even in the most unlikely places. With my prompting, he searched in a distant warehouse and discovered that high-quality copies of my originals were stored there. We sent those materials to my new manufacturer to use, and I was happily back in business. A difficult week was averted and my major account saved.

2. Take a Mini-Break

If you're having one of those days and are feeling over-whelmed by work or circumstances, give yourself a few minutes to regroup. In situations like these, you especially need to stay centered and to get comfortably back on track. One way to do this is to take a brief mental vacation to a lovely place where you once felt peaceful.

Your imagined mini-vacation might be drifting in a boat on a mountain lake, walking in a beautiful meadow, or visiting a favorite friend. By involving all your senses and taking several deep breaths, you can recreate the memory and enjoy the experience again.

In this relaxed state while you're on 'vacation,' think about all the times that you felt enthused, excited about being alive, and really connected to your Higher Self. Remembering times when you felt confident, creative, and positive will help you to recreate that frame of mind.

When you return from your mini-vacation, you'll be refreshed, alert, and ready to tackle what you want to do.

3. There's No Rush Hour in Heaven

In the universe, things happen in a natural progression when the time is right. The seasons follow each other in a predictable sequence, the Earth continues to revolve about the sun, and plants and animals obey their natural cycles.

Likewise, when you're having a great day, things go smoothly. You seem to be in the right place at the right time. You're happy, positive, and full of energy.

Sometimes, however, problems arise and seem to throw off your timing. Feeling impatient or frustrated may only throw off your timing even more. In this case, it's important to get back in tune with your Inner Knowing.

To do this, center yourself with a meditation or with a mini-vacation as described above. During this time acknowledge Spirit's presence in your life and affirm that you are one with It. Know that everything you need happens in the perfect order and the perfect time for the good of all involved. This doesn't suggest that you remain passive, but rather that you proceed with confidence in a relaxed way. Spirit can then work through you and enable you to think clearly and act instead of react.

All the good in the universe is available to you at any time, and when you act in alignment with Spirit, something as good as what you have, or better, is in the works and on its way to you.

Thus fortified by positive thinking, you can take further steps to salvage a difficult day by doing the following.

4. Focus on Your More Significant Items

This is always an excellent rule to follow, but it is especially important on difficult days. When you spend at least some time on a significant item you can look back and realize that, even though the day was rough, you at least made some headway. This gives you a greater feeling of control and a greater sense of accomplishment.

One way to determine the significance of an item is to ask what's the best that will happen if you finish a particular item and what's the worst that will happen if you don't. Weigh the consequences and act accordingly.

5. Increase Your Concentration

To better focus on the important task at hand, avoid impulse chores such as making unnecessary phone calls.

Hang a sign on your door that says, "Please come in only in case of an emergency." If you and your co-workers share an office, and it isn't realistic to close the door, consider putting three small flags on each desk: a red flag that signals, "Interrupt me only if there's an emergency," a yellow or orange flag that signals, "Caution. Interrupt me if you must, but it better be important," and a green flag that gives the go-ahead, "Talk to me if you need to."

Sweep the clutter off your desk and put it out of sight. You'll feel lighter and more mentally alert.

Save low-priority items for another time. Plan a trivia session for some time when you don't feel like handling anything major or starting anything new. At this time quickly deal with whatever has accumulated.

After an interruption—telephone call, drop-in visitor, fire alarm, coffee break, whatever—return to your work and quickly restore your concentraiton by taking a few deep, cleansing breaths and repeating your mantra or code word as described in Chapter 1. Then remind yourself of your mission statement to help yourself stay on track.

6. Revise What You Need to Do

Determine which items on your to-do list you can salvage and which you can postpone. On some items, you can do the minimum that's required to move them to the next stage. If you promised people a report, for example, but you're going to be late, give them a quick update: what you've done so far and when they can expect the rest. You also might consider giving them a draft of the report. This way, you don't abandon people who are counting on you, you buy yourself more time, and you may prevent others from having one of 'those' days.

7. Negotiate Deadlines

If you're in danger of missing a deadline, let others know as soon as possible in order to minimize any inconvenience to them, and ask if you can move back the deadline. Communicating with people, even if the news is 'bad,' shows that you're sincere and helps you maintain your professional credibility.

8. Analyze Why the Day Was Difficult

When one of 'those' days is finally over, evaluate what went wrong. Then find ways to prevent future difficult days, such as giving yourself more lead time on projects, taking a time-management class, delegating more, being more assertive, redefining your goals, staying 'prayed up' so you can draw on your reservoir of inner strength and intuition in time of challenges.

9. Get the Big Picture

Ask yourself how this one day is going to fit in with the rest of your life. For every tough day that you have, you have many more that run smoothly.

When you align yourself with a Higher Power, act with confidence, concentrate on your most significant items, expect the best, and give thanks for all the great days that you've already had, you're sure to see many of them.

"If my problems have brought me to prayer, then they have served a purpose."

Al-Anon Family Group Staff, As We Understood

■

"If you understand, things are just as they are; if you do not understand, things are just as they are."

Zen proverb

■

"The trivialities of every day, the disappointments and the petty annoyances and the hurts you allow yourselves to receive from daily life, are all very small; but you yourselves allow them to seem very big. Let them recede, concentrate your whole being upon the love of God."

White Eagle, The Quiet Mind

■

"The ability to simplify means to eliminate the unnecessary so that the necessary may speak."

Hans Hoffmann

■

"We are not victims of the world, but victims of the way we perceive the world."

Carol Record, Unity minister

■

"Don't sweat the small stuff; and remember, it's all small stuff."

Author Unknown

■

"When one is natural he is relaxed within and able to accept what life offers."

The Great Religions of the World (Taoism)

Chapter 9

The Business of Being Positive

"If you have any questions,
please do not hesitate to call."

THE SENTENCE above is the most commonly used close in business writing today and is written with the best of intentions. But it can be worded much more effectively, as you'll soon discover.

Language Shapes Our Experiences

The earliest lesson that many of us learn when we first become interested in self-improvement is to express ourselves in positive terms. This is because the language that we use, which reflects our beliefs, helps to shape our experiences. Being positive also serves us well at work, where we want to encourage cooperation, make sales, serve customers well, produce quality products, and earn our salary or make a good profit.

It's important to note, however, that some casual negative comments are just that—casual and innocent. "This cheesecake is to die for!" for example, uses the idiom *to die for*. This is probably a fairly harmless statement, although some health-food enthusiasts might think that it's prophetic. What the speaker really means is, "This cheesecake is incredibly delicious!"

There are also times when a negative is simply a declarative statement: "They don't want to go there." Again, fairly harmless. Other times speakers use negatives because it's easier than taking time to think about how to express a thought in a more positive way—even though being positive usually saves time.

On the other hand, some negative comments that appear to be casual on the surface are actually fueled by negative emotions. These negatives, used on a regular basis, can produce unwanted results in a speaker's outward experience. The comment "They're filthy rich," for example, could mean that the speaker is envious of someone else or maybe thinking, "At least *someone* can make that kind of money; it may not be *me*, but *someone* can!" This is quite a strong—and pessimistic—affirmation, which, if used over time, could interfere with the speaker's financial success.

So the challenge for you as a communicator is to notice which of the negatives you use are simply casual and innocent, and which are produced by strong negative emotions, 'negative' because they might sabotage your success. Also notice if these particular negatives are part of an ongoing pattern of negativity. If this is the case, you might want to put a more positive spin on your communication.

Proof Positive

Research studies document the fact that being positive helps us to communicate more clearly with others.

1. It's easier for people to understand and remember positive sentences because it's easier to *visualize* positives. The command "Don't walk on the grass," for example, immediately draws our attention to the grass and conjures up

images of walking on it. The human brain has trouble processing and visualizing a 'don't.' So to communicate a clear picture of what you do want from people and to increase your chances of getting results, you might say, "Please use the walk."

2. Being positive saves time and is more direct than being negative. Positive sentences, both written and spoken, are usually shorter than negative sentences. The sentence "Use positives" is shorter than the sentence "Don't use negatives."

3. People are usually more receptive to your ideas when you're positive. To illustrate this point, think about someone you know who's usually positive and upbeat compared to someone you know who's pessimistic. How do you feel when you're with each of these people? Chances are, when you spend time with the positive person, you feel energized, enthused, and open to his or her ideas. Likewise you'll tend to affect people favorably when *you're* positive.

4. You feel better when you're positive. You can prove this to yourself by remembering a pleasant experience that you've had. Involve all your senses in the memory and notice how good you feel.

Now that you cannot *not* understand what I'm saying, let's move on. Or in other words: now that you understand what I'm saying, let's move on.

Avoid the Three Categories of Negative Words

To keep your communication positive, avoid the following three categories of negative words: obviously negative words, words with negative meanings, and double negatives or potentially confusing negatives.

Obviously Negative Words

These negative words are the easiest to avoid because they're so evident. They are words such as *don't, can't, won't, not,* and *no.* Replace obviously negative words with statements of what you do want. Notice that in every case that follows, the positive sentences are shorter and more to the point than the negative sentences.

Negative	Positive
The new rule will not prevent you from making changes.	The new rule lets you make changes.
You can't miss it.	You'll find it.
Don't forget to register.	Remember to register.

Words with Negative Meanings

It's also easy to avoid using words with negative implications such as *reject, failure, mistake, limit, hesitate, doubt,* and *complain.* To be a more positive communicator, replace words that may have negative meanings with words that have positive meanings. This is especially important if you want to foster teamwork or get results from customers, clients, co-workers, and others in the workplace.

Negative	Positive
This corrects the mistake that you made in your account.	Your account is now current.
We'll give careful attention to your complaint.	We'll do our best to serve you.
Avoid using negatives.	Use positives.
You won't fail.	You'll succeed.
I don't expect any opposition from them.	I'm sure they'll cooperate.

Double Negatives or Confusing Negatives

A double negative is the use of two or more negatives to express a single negative. Double negatives, in fact, actually express a positive. "I don't know nothing about the subject," for example, technically means that you *do* know something about it. What you probably mean is that you know nothing about it.

An even more subtle and potentially confusing negative occurs when you start to say one thing, then, in mid-sentence, reverse what you're saying. For example, "Don't use this exit except in emergencies." The first part of the sentence, "Don't use this exit," sets up one command, then negates it by saying "except in emergencies." This sentence actually means, "Use this exit only in emergencies."

To keep your communication clear, avoid using double and confusing negatives.

Negative	Positive
I don't know nothing.	I know something (or, I know nothing).
In all cases except one . . .	In most cases . . .
Do not call unless you have questions.	Call if you have questions.
He was not promoted until he filled out the paperwork.	He was promoted when he filled out the paperwork.

Beware of Hidden Negatives

Is your communication peppered with hidden negatives? To weed out negative thinking at the deepest levels, be sure to use positive communication in the two following categories: casual conversation and embedded suggestions.

Casual Conversation

Hidden negatives can slip into the most casual conversation. You may recognize some of the expressions below from conversations you've heard or had.

Negative	Positive
I'm dying for a raise.	I'd love a raise.
It's killing me not to know.	I want to know.
He's a pain in the neck.	He's a real challenge.

Embedded Suggestions

An embedded suggestion is a command that's enclosed within a spoken or a written sentence. Because the suggestion is concealed, people's defenses may be down. The suggestion can go directly into their unconscious minds without being censored.

In the sentence "I really feel tired today, Sally," the speaker seems to be referring to himself or herself. When the listener, in this case Sally, hears the word *tired*, she begins to form associations of what *tired* means to her. And, as we know, what we think about tends to multiply. By the same token, if a speaker says, "I really feel great today, Sally," the speaker is embedding a suggestion for Sally to feel as good as the speaker does.

A single embedded suggestion may have little effect on a listener or a reader. If a speaker or a writer uses a variety of similar suggestions over a period of time, however, the suggestions may have a cumulative effect. The listener or the reader may begin to feel tired or energized accordingly.

You can find embedded suggestions—negative and positive—in all human communication. Responsible people, however, strive to be positive and to influence with integrity. In the following sentences, the embedded suggestions are italicized.

> When I spend time with positive people, I *feel energized and enthused*.

> It would be smart for you to *support this plan*.

> Since there are often two ways to say the same thing, you'll be ahead of the game if *you choose the positive*.

"If You Have Any Questions . . ."

Now let's look at the sentence *If you have any questions, please do not hesitate to call*.

1. The word *hesitate* can have negative connotations. To hesitate usually means to falter, waver, vacillate, flounder, or delay. You can replace *hesitate* with a more affirmative phrase that suggests action: *please call.*
2. The embedded suggestion "do not *hesitate to call*" subtly suggests that readers hesitate to call. Remember, the mind has trouble visualizing a 'don't.'
3. The sentence is a cliché nowadays. Just about everyone uses it or has used it.
4. The phrase "Do not" is an obvious negative. It's more effective to state what you do want—*please call*—rather than what you do not want.

Does this evaluation sound picky? After all, people are just being polite when they say, "If you have any questions, please do not hesitate to call." This is a perfectly good, gracious—and acceptable—way to sign a letter. It also represents what happens on a grand scale in a lot of business writing these days. People sometimes communicate unconsciously, take the path of least resistance, or use well-worn phrases to save time.

A more effective way to close a letter is to use stronger words that suggest action. You could say, "If you have questions, please call." Or you could get even more mileage out of your close. You could personalize it or make it more conversational by saying something like:

- Sally, we're looking forward to working with you.
- I trust you'll find this information helpful.
- See you soon.
- Armando, thanks for your attention.
- I'm looking forward to hearing from you.
- Thanks again, Ms. Niendorff, for all your help.
- We appreciate your business.
- Best wishes, Rachel, and continued success.
- Call us today and we'll rush your order.

- All the best.
- Mr. Levitz, you can trust us to do the job right.
- See you at the meeting.
- We'll help in any way we can.

How to Communicate More Consciously

A great time to practice positive communication is when you write letters, memos, or reports. This is because you can think about what you're writing and revise what you've written. You might want to study copies of letters you've already sent and figure out how to be more positive the next time. And after every letter you write and every e-mail you're about to send, glance through it to make sure you've worded your message in a positive way.

The more positive you are when you write, the easier it'll be for you to be positive when you speak. You might also become more aware of the negatives others use. As you listen to people, you might want to turn their negatives into positives in your mind. If someone says, "Don't forget the meeting," think to yourself, "Remember the meeting."

Choose Success

Good communication, spoken or written, is the basis of every successful business transaction. When you apply the ideas in this chapter you'll communicate your message to listeners or readers clearly and simply in the quickest amount of time. You'll enhance your professional image as well as the image of your company. You'll feel more positive about yourself, and what you communicate will get results.

"Better keep yourself clean and bright; you are the window through which you must see the world."

George Bernard Shaw

"There is a power above and behind us and we are the channel of its communication."

Ralph Waldo Emerson

"What we love we shall grow to resemble."

Bernard of Clairvaux

"The best way to cheer yourself up is to try to cheer somebody else up."

Mark Twain

"Most of the shadows in this life are caused by standing in one's own sunshine."

Ralph Waldo Emerson

"Start by doing what's necessary; then do what's possible; and suddenly you are doing the impossible."

St. Francis of Assisi

"I never lost a game. I just ran out of time."

Bobby Layne, pro-football player

"It may be those who do most, dream most."

Stephen Leacock

"Every good thought you think is contributing its share to the ultimate result of your life."

Grenville Kleiser

"Let one therefore keep the mind pure, for what a man thinks, that he becomes."

The Upanishads

"Sometimes it is necessary to reteach a thing its loveliness . . . until it flowers again from within."

Galway Kinnell

Chapter 10

No Bankruptcy in Heaven

AT FIRST I didn't take losing most of my money very gracefully. Maybe that's because it happened the same week I lost my job and my apartment.

I'd quit a regular job—at the detoxification center mentioned in Chapter 6—to take a chance on a business venture with a man who was beginning his own seminar company. I hadn't worked for him for very long when one day he called to inform me that he couldn't use my services any more. Nor could he afford to pay me for the work I'd already done or reimburse me for the travel expenses I'd already paid myself. He was on the verge of bankruptcy. Furthermore, he'd scheduled me to work in one more city. If I went, I'd be teaching for free.

Three days later my landlord notified me that he wanted the apartment where I lived for his nephew. I had to vacate the premises by the end of the month. With a 2 percent vacancy rate at that time in San Francisco, where I was living, and with little savings and no job, I faced a grim search for a new place to live.

Caught in a Rip Tide

The next two weeks were bleak and frightening. I wandered dazed through the city feeling as though I'd been caught in a rip tide and was being sucked out to sea and dragged under.

About the third week, I realized that this was the perfect opportunity to apply spiritual principles about faith, trust, and prosperity. I only wish that I'd had a spiritual response sooner and saved myself a lot of misery.

The True Source of Supply

I realized that all the apparent loss and upheaval in my life might be a sign that the time had come to move on, an indication that I needed a new beginning. Something was reorganizing my life and I had to have faith that the changes would be beneficial to me in some way I was yet to discover. I had to trust that with spiritual guidance I'd be safe wherever I went, whatever I did.

After some deliberation, I decided to move to Texas with a business associate who owned property there. As a freelance writer and an independent business consultant, I could live anywhere I wanted.

Next I examined the idea of 'bankruptcy.' To be bankrupt was to be financially ruined. It certainly seemed that my former employer was ruined, but I'd never considered him a failure, nor did I consider myself a failure. We were creative individuals with a divine surplus of prosperity, energy, and ideas. Just because the circumstances seemed devastating, we personally did not need to feel devastated.

Then I affirmed that Spirit is the source of my supply, not one particular person or job. I was confident that some day, somehow, I'd be compensated either by my former employer or in some other way. And I released the idea of ever seeing the money. This was a giant step for someone who used to keep a mental tally of everything that people owed her. I also elected to make, at my own expense, the business trip he'd already scheduled for me, and I spent what I thought was my last day of work in the exciting city of New Orleans.

Fast Food—or Feast?

That evening as I wondered where to eat dinner, someone pointed out that there was a fast-food restaurant across the street. I had also noticed Sazerac, an elegant restaurant downstairs in the hotel. Eating there would cost much more than eating fast food across the street. What I did next would be a crucial affirmation of my faith in a greater power—or my lack of faith.

I wanted a symbol for my belief that things would be all right, and, while I wasn't about to commit myself to payments on a luxury car, I did think that a nice dinner was in order. So, affirming that there is no bankruptcy in heaven, I dressed up and went downstairs to eat at Sazerac.

There I dined leisurely in quiet elegance, surrounded by warm ruby tones, pale pink tablecloths, golden plates, crystal, mahogany, and damask. Six waiters served me. I feasted on gourmet delights and between courses cleansed my palate with lime sorbet served in a carved-ice swan bordered with sugared grapes. Having emotionally released the whole complicated mess of employment and salaries and money owed, I focused on my move to Texas.

But when I returned to San Francisco after my business trip, my 'former' employer telephoned to say that he'd found investors for his company. In just a month's time things had turned around. He wanted to continue using my consulting services, and he was able to pay me everything that he had owed me before I left San Francisco.

I continued to work for him but still moved to the Dallas/ Forth Worth area to live, because I'd put that plan in motion.

And because I traveled extensively throughout the country working for him, it didn't matter where I lived. But now I moved with the knowledge that the new beginning I'd needed was not a move to another state in the country, but rather a move to another state of consciousness. It had taken the threat of bankruptcy to move me to a higher level of trust and faith.

I'd learned a valuable lesson that has served me well ever since: circumstances always change; the availability of Spirit is the only constant. When all seems to have been lost, we still have the indwelling Light to inspire, guide, and nourish us. Even though we may let doubts and fears seem to obscure It, nothing can endanger that safe, eternal place within us.

The things we think, say, and do almost always involve either an affirmation or a denial of this greater Power. So the next time you have an important choice about whether to believe in limitation or abundance, choose divine abundance. Choose Sazerac.

■

"Do not look where you fell, but where you slipped."
Liberian proverb

■

"The mind grows by what it feeds on."
Josiah G. Holland

■

"To grow spiritually, you do not need to create a perfect environment, have no negativity around you, or retreat from the world. You are here to learn how to be your Higher Self in the midst of the kinds of energies that are present on earth."
Sanaya Roman

■

"I have learned that when your inner helper is in charge, do not try to think consciously. Drift—wait—and obey."
Rudyard Kipling

■

"Obstacles are what you see when you take your eyes off the goal."
Author Unknown

■

"When it gets dark enough, you can see the stars."
Charles A. Beard

■

Chapter 11

How to Deal with Difficult Behavior in the Workplace

Angry. Sullen. Hostile. Cranky. Abrupt. Withdrawn. Stubborn. Irrational. Manipulative. Negative.

Do ANY of the words above describe someone you know at work? Maybe a customer or a client? Maybe your boss, partner, employee, or co-worker?

Even though we all share a common spiritual core, we each have different life experiences that continue to shape us as individuals. In the process of living, people sometimes let circumstances upset them. They consequently may feel frustrated, angry, depressed, or other emotions that we might consider difficult. This behavior can thwart or complicate our best intentions at work.

How can you keep a positive perspective when less-than-professional behavior bogs down business? Here are 12 ideas to help you smooth the way to successful resolutions.

1. First ask what you can *know* about a situation, then what you can do about it. Know that we're all in the process of

growing as human beings. Once you establish that common connection and the shared goal of evolving spiritually, it's easier to be guided by the indwelling Spirit and take the appropriate action.

2. Realize that difficult behavior may be someone's bid for understanding, love, or acceptance. The more difficult the behavior, the more desperate the bid. It might be a cry for help, not an assault on you personally.

3. Separate the behavior from the person. You can care about people even though you don't like, or approve of, some of the things they do.

4. Remember that people usually rationalize their behavior no matter what it is. To challenge them, threaten them, or disagree with them might only make them more defensive and more stubborn. So rather than trying to convince others that they're wrong and you're right, approach the problem with a cooperative spirit of looking for solutions.

5. Find common ground on which to agree. When you agree with people, they feel that you understand them, at least in part, and may be more receptive to your ideas. Common ground between you and a customer who is irate, for example, might be good service: the customer wants it and you want to provide it. Assure the customer of your intentions to give good service. Acknowledge any problems, apologize if necessary, but don't demean yourself; then express your willingness to remedy the situation. You might say something like, "I'm sorry this happened. Here's what I'm going to do to correct the situation and prevent future problems," or, "You're right, this has been a problem. Let's figure out a way to fix it. Any ideas?"

6. Avoid judging people by your own standards, which may be inappropriate or unrealistic to the situation or unfair to people. If you work long hours, for example, you might be suspicious of people who take frequent breaks or go home right at closing every evening. Or you might judge

people for using poor grammar even though English may be their second language or they may not be responsible for written communication in the company. Then there's always the possibility you don't know the real reasons why people do what they do.

7. Avoid mind-reading. When you think you've figured out why someone is acting a certain way, you might say something like, "Here's what seems to be happening. Is that what's really going on?" Their answers might surprise you. For example, Susan got the feeling that Joe didn't like her because he was often abrupt with her. Since it was *her* style to be abrupt with people when she was angry at them, she concluded that Joe was mad at her. One day, rather than assuming the worst, she said to Joe, "I get the feeling that you're angry at me. Are you?" It turned out that Joe wasn't even aware he was being abrupt. He simply thought he was being efficient and doing his job quickly. If Joe had been angry with Susan, she had given him an opportunity to share his feelings and resolve any differences.

8. Avoid asking 'why' questions, which people often interpret as combative. Instead, ask, "What's going on?" "How do you feel about this?" or "Can you tell me more about it?"

9. Talk in terms of your thoughts and feelings rather than accuse others. Instead of saying, "You're always late with the monthly report," you might say something like, "I can plan my presentation on time for the staff meetings if I know I'll have your report by the first of each month. Can I count on you?"

10. Realize that people interpret behavior differently. You might think that someone is nagging you, for example, when the other person thinks that he or she is just trying to be helpful. Or someone who seems to be unmotivated simply may not know, or understand, the company policy or where he or she fits into the big picture. Again, one of the faster ways to smooth out communication is to tell

others what you've observed and ask if that's what's really going on.

11. Think about how the objectionable behavior might serve the people engaged in it and find a way to help them meet those needs more constructively. People who gossip, for example, might be trying to get attention or to appear interesting. So help them fill their needs constructively by reinforcing their positive personality traits and giving them well-deserved recognition.

12. Use the "Olé!" technique described by Peter Turla, president of the National Management Institute, a training and consulting firm in the Dallas/Fort Worth area. "When people are being difficult I use the technique that bullfighters use when a bull charges them. I mentally step aside and think, 'Olé!' I let them blow off steam, then direct them to positive solutions. I might ask, 'What can we do to correct the problem?' or 'What would have to happen for you to feel good about this?' This way I show them that I care. And when I look beyond their behavior to what they want, we tend to resolve things quickly."

Once you put things in perspective, here are some specific strategies that you can use if you confront various types of difficult behavior.

Hostile Behavior

1. If someone is creating a scene, stay calm and guard against an angry knee-jerk reaction. Most people cool off in a matter of minutes if you don't antagonize them.

2. Realize that the person may be yelling at the situation rather than at you. He or she may have personal problems. While this doesn't excuse others from being rude, it may help you to emerge from the fray with your ego intact.

3. Once the person calms down, paraphrase the problem to show that you've been listening.
4. Steer the conversation toward solutions. Complaints often indicate that something is wrong. Ask for ideas, suggestions, and recommendations. You may discover solutions that you hadn't considered.

Noncommunicative Behavior

1. Ask leading questions to encourage people to share their feelings. If their answers are abrupt, persist with open-ended questions such as "Tell me more about it."
2. If they don't respond at all, ask, "What's going on? I'd like to know so we can straighten this out." Sometimes you need to convince people that you genuinely care about them before they'll open up to you.
3. Be nonjudgmental. Make it safe for others to share their feelings.

Negative Behavior

1. Instead of playing 'ain't it awful!' with people, acknowledge their feelings and state your willingness to explore solutions. For example, say, "If that's a problem, what can we do about it?"
2. If someone complains to you about someone else, emphasize the fact that telling you about it won't solve anything. Suggest that the person complaining talk to the other person or people involved.

Meddlesome Behavior

1. If people give you advice on how to solve your problems, keep an open mind and listen. They may sincerely want to help and might have some valid suggestions.

2. If they persist in telling you what to do and it begins to feel like they're interfering, say something like, "I appreciate your help, but I want to work this out on my own for the learning experience" or "Thanks for your suggestions. I'll consider them."

Uncooperative Behavior

1. Motivate people for an assignment by telling them what's in it for them and emphasize how important their contribution is to the overall project.
2. Ask for their opinions, recommendations, and advice. Make them feel needed. They are!
3. Clarify the company's rules and policies so that people understand what's expected of them.
4. Encourage constructive grievances. Uncooperative behavior may indicate that something needs to be changed.
5. Reward people for work well done. Give ample credit and well-deserved acknowledgment, raises, promotions, or letters of thanks. Your recognition and appreciation may be the perfect incentive to get people to cooperate.

What to Do if People Think *You're* Difficult

If you're surrounded by people who are being difficult, realize that they may be reacting, in part, to something that *you're* doing. If your behavior seems to bother people and you want things to run more smoothly in the office or in the department, ask for tactful reminders when they think that you're being difficult. If, for example, your perfectionism tends to slow down relatively unimportant matters, invite others to make you aware of when you're doing this.

Take 'Ten'

Whenever you want to communicate with someone, set some time aside for a focused, uninterrupted discussion. People may be more willing to talk with you if they feel they have your full attention. Taking ten minutes, or however much time you need, can actually save you time that otherwise might have been lost because of misunderstandings.

When you keep the lines of communication open, you can handle differences quickly and effectively with compassion and understanding. You'll more fully express your spiritual nature and acknowledge it in others. And you'll get back to work faster and in a more positive frame of mind.

■

"I always prefer to believe the best of everybody—it saves so much trouble."

Rudyard Kipling

■

"The best way to knock a chip off someone's shoulder is to give him or her a pat on the back."

Author Unknown

■

"One who loves God finds the object of his love everywhere."

Sri Aurobindo, The Life Divine

■

"A man has as many social selves as there are individuals who recognize him and carry an image around of him in their mind."

William James

■

"Patience is the key to paradise."

Turkish proverb

■

"They who throw dirt lose ground."

Author Unknown

■

"One way to avoid criticism is to do nothing and to be a nobody. The world will then not bother you."

Napoleon Hill

■

"In things spiritual, there is no partition, no number, no individuals. How sweet is the oneness—unearth the treasure of Unity."

Rumi, Masnavi

■

Chapter 12

How to Deal with the Ethically Challenged

I WILL do whatever it takes to succeed in business—*whatever*!'' a woman told me. Her eyes had a cold glint and a fierce determination that made me pray never to encounter her in a business situation. I was so unnerved by her uncompromising position, in fact, that I didn't even ask what business she was in.

It seems she was leaving her options open to be either deliberately unethical or inadvertently unethical: to break the law in an obvious way or just let things slide. People who are inadvertently unethical don't take the time to treat others fairly or with respect; they may be so caught up in getting ahead or so overwhelmed with work that their consciences are missing in action, so to speak.

If people have treated you unfairly, it's good to first get your ego out of the way: meditate or pray; go for a walk or a run; write an angry letter to the other party, then tear it up without mailing it or give it to a more objective colleague to edit. This can help you keep things in perspective. Then, in a more positive frame of mind, you can do what you need to do to improve the situation.

"*Whatever* It Takes!"

In a way it's easier to deal with blatantly unethical behavior, because the transgressions are so obvious—as in the two cases below.

The Case of the Property (Mis)manager

Paul hired Ron to manage some rental property for him. Ron, a previously unemployed repair man, went to collect the rent and apparently saw an opportunity to make a fast buck. He told the renters that he needed the money in cash, then didn't deposit the money in Paul's account. When Paul called Ron's home, Ron's wife said that he was out of town and she didn't know when he'd be back.

What's a clean, effective way to handle this situation? Paul didn't waste his time and energy judging Ron for stealing or judging *himself* for making a bad hiring decision. Nor did he sit around wringing his hands and wondering why people couldn't be more honest. Instead, he told Ron's wife that he was going to have the police issue a warrant for Ron's arrest. She somehow got the message to Ron and he returned the money. The situation was resolved quickly, Ron was given an opportunity to redeem himself, and Paul hired a more ethical property manager.

The Cost of an Education

Years ago I invested some money with an oil tycoon—we'll call him Dewey—who showed the investors photographs of oil gushing forth from 'our' wells. It sure looked good, but then one of the investors noticed that Dewey's office seemed only temporary, as though scaled down for a quick getaway. Turns out Dewey *was* ethically impaired. The investors began to realize that fact and things got nasty. Threats were made, clandestine meetings were held, and Dewey's right-hand man was thrown through a window in the style of an old, Wild West barroom brawl.

The investors entered a class-action suit against Dewey, which ended with our attorney cleaning up—for himself. We never saw a cent of our money. Then we got to battle the attorney to get him to reduce his inflated fees.

My emotions ran the gamut. I was upset that I lost money, then angry at Dewey and embarrassed that I'd been so gullible. I was also proud to have stood up for my rights as an investor and confronted the attorney, who finally adjusted his fees more fairly.

I eventually bailed out of the mess $8000 'poorer' financially, but I gained a valuable $8000 education. I'd learned to research potential investments thoroughly, investigate the credibility of the people involved, diversify my investments, and let go of resentment. The rip-off had happened. I'd dealt with it, learned from it, and moved on.

In all endeavors it's necessary to recognize the point of diminishing returns, the point at which the gain on your invested time, money, or energy no longer exceeds the value of your investment. Sheri, in the following example, found herself trapped in a difficult situation and paid a tremendous price.

To Sue or Not to Sue

Sheri had done some extra work for her boss with the understanding that he'd pay her for working overtime, but when payday came there was no additional compensation. So she quit her job and hired a team of attorneys to sue her former boss. The case dragged on and on for several years, and the attorneys didn't seem to be making any progress. Sheri depleted her savings to pay her legal fees, than began to withdraw money from her retirement fund to continue to pay them.

When she ran out of money, her attorneys dropped her case saying they'd done all that they could for her. Meanwhile, her former boss, apparently a well-liked man known for his generosity, seemed unscathed. Sheri felt betrayed and demoralized, never saw a penny of the money she felt she was due, and never recovered any of the money she'd paid in legal fees. The incident left her bitter, depressed, and profoundly exhausted.

Her case was never settled. Many cases, though, are settled out of court, but only after huge legal costs and fees are paid, creativity diverted, goals put on hold, time and energy spent, and emotions held hostage for the duration of the long ordeal.

If you're facing a situation that calls for legal action, consider what it'll cost you in time, emotion, and money. Is it best to tie up your energy in a lawsuit or instead to invest it in moving forward with your life? If you decide that legal action is necessary, consider the option of going to a good mediator, found in the telephone book under "Arbitration," "Mediation," "Conflict Resolution," or "Dispute Resolution."

In such a mediation, both sides submit their views of the dispute to a trained, objective counselor experienced in conflict management. The parties are directly involved in defining the terms of the settlement in an informal, confidential setting. Many cases are settled in just two or three days and, in some cases, in two or three hours. There are no depositions, judges, juries, attorneys, or exorbitant legal fees. Time, energy, money, and dignity are saved on both sides.

How do lawyers feel about mediations? At first many of them were afraid that it would adversely affect their business, but now growing numbers are taking mediation training themselves. They're riding the horse in the direction it's going, so to speak—toward a friendlier, less expensive way of resolving differences.

Missing in Action

An example of inadvertent unethical behavior is the literary agent who kept an author's manuscript for almost eight months—thereby keeping it out of the marketplace—and finally returned it with virtually no comment. Let's call her Joanne.

Every time the author, Lilly, called for a status report during the long wait, Joanne's assistant told her that Joanne was extremely busy, sick, or out of town, and they'd have a decision next week. "Next week" turned into seven-and-a-half months. Yet the assistant continued to assure Lilly that her manuscript was "perfect for us. . . . Joanne loves it. . . . we think it's going to be a winner" and "It's still in our 'hot' file." All this encouragement lulled Lilly into a false sense of security. She figured it was a done deal and didn't seek representation elsewhere.

After seven-and-a-half months Joanne finally had time to meet Lilly, but by then Lilly had run out of patience. And as the saying goes, "People count the faults of those who keep them waiting."

The meeting didn't go well. Lilly was guardedly impatient and Joanne was recovering from pneumonia. She gave Lilly a contract to read but not to sign until Joanne gave her the go-ahead. A week later Joanne returned the manuscript with no comment other than, "Please do not be discouraged with your project. It has great potential; however, we simply do not have the ability to take on a project of this kind at this time."

They didn't have the "ability"—meaning the time, the staff, the connections? To take on "a project of this kind"—meaning inspirational, philosophical, metaphysical? "At this time"—meaning this month, this year, this lifetime? Lilly called Joanne's office several times to ask for specifics, which Lilly felt she deserved to know because she'd waited so long for a decision, but she couldn't get past the receptionist. And no one ever got back to her.

Lilly felt bitter and bruised—Joanne had kept her manuscript off the market for months, led her on, betrayed her trust, and possibly destroyed her chances of selling the book—but Lilly also felt some relief. If Joanne had treated her that badly when Lilly supposedly had something she wanted, a winning manuscript, how would Joanne have treated her if Lilly had signed a contract with her?

So there Lilly was trying to conduct business in good faith, and expecting others to do the same, and someone came along and ran right over her. What to do? Here are some ideas that you might find helpful if you find yourself in a similar situation.

To Be Spiritual Means to Be Strong

Some people think that being spiritual means to put yourself at risk of being taken advantage of and, if that happens, to submissively 'turn the other cheek.' I personally think it's spiritual to be confident and assertive. It's spiritual to stand up for your rights, to remind others that you're a worthy individual, and to hold people accountable for their behavior. You *deserve* to be respected! When you assert yourself, other people have an opportunity to make things right or, at least, to realize that their actions have consequences.

1. Restore Your Faith in Yourself

If you've been betrayed or misled in business, you might first be angry at the people you feel were responsible and then, at some point, question your own judgment, "How could I have been so gullible?" In Lilly's case, she was alternately furious at Joanne for causing the apparent demise of her manuscript and angry at herself for believing Joanne's stalling tactics and letting her have such a long, exclusive look at it.

Rather than condemn yourself for having become ensnared in a difficult situation, it's healthier to comfort yourself. You've been hurt. Don't make matters worse by beating yourself up; instead, console yourself. Remember all the smart decisions you've made in the past, all the ethical people you know, all that you've accomplished, and *everything* that's working for you right now. Then remember a time you achieved something you wanted—recognition, a raise or promotion, an award, an important account—and bask in those memories. This helps you to repair your faith in yourself, takes the sting out of a temporary defeat, and helps you put things in perspective—good things *do* happen to you.

2. Look for the Spiritual Laws Influencing the Events

Remember that nothing happens in isolation. Take an objective look at what went wrong. You're an integral part of the whole and, in one way or another, a crucial player in every situation you encounter. In Lilly's case, she questioned if she was responsible, in part, for what had happened with Joanne, and she looked for ways to do things differently the next time.

After a few months of waiting for Joanne's decision, Lilly could have told her that she was going to send her manuscript to other agents as well. The fear of loss might have motivated Joanne to overcome her procrastination, which Lilly had allowed to continue. Now because of her hard-earned lesson, Lilly calls people earlier for status reports and allows editors exclusive consideration of her work only if they can tell her by when they'll have a decision. When that time arrives, if they're still procrastinating, Lilly moves on with a clear conscience.

As hard as it was for her to release a situation in which she'd had almost an eight-month investment of time and energy, she knew she had to. But things felt so unfinished. Then she reminded herself that nothing is ever truly finished, just transformed. So she let go of her anger and shortly after found a publisher for her book.

3. Ask if the Future Would 'Fit'

Ask yourself if any part of you might be resisting change, even a positive one. Someone once told me that maybe the reason she never won when she played Bingo was that she was too shy to go up on stage in front of everyone to receive the prize. She suspected that some part of her may have known that and sabotaged her success.

In Lilly's case, there may have been things that Lilly did not want to do had Joanne represented her. Some of Joanne's authors, for instance, had become celebrities with their own talk-shows. Lilly didn't want a talk-show. Had she signed a contract with Joanne, this might have become a point of contention between them. Joanne might have wanted her to be more ambitious.

She also knew what presentation style best represented her material. Many of Joanne's authors were flamboyant public personalities with their names in flashing lights on the stage behind them. Not Lilly's style. She wanted her material to speak for itself, not the theatrics.

4. More Power to Them

For a while Lilly felt a special satisfaction whenever one of Joanne's authors received a bad book review or had a television show canceled. But Lilly had to admit, with some embarrassment, that her reaction to their misfortune was her own desire in disguise. If she'd had the success she felt she deserved, she wouldn't have been so preoccupied with other people's losses—or their successes.

"When you win, nothing hurts," football-great Joe Namath once said. To expand on that idea, when people feel truly successful, they tend to be more cheerful and forgiving. If you've been resenting other people's successes, practice saying, "Good for you! More power to you. More power and success to *everyone* including myself."

5. Use Sharks to Your Advantage

I'm not talking about the ocean variety of sharks, I'm talking about 'paper sharks'—those people who call and say they're from my photocopier company and they need to know the model number of my machine. What they're intending to do is send me poorly made or overpriced supplies that I haven't ordered. They're hoping that I'll think someone else in the company ordered them and pay for them without questioning the invoice. A few well-placed questions—what did you say your name is, what's your phone number, don't you have that information if you're from our copier company?—results in their hanging up.

An updated version of this scam is the 'shark' who sends people copies of their own Web pages and an invoice for a particular amount. The enclosed letter states that the "unsolicited advertisement" arrived at the shark's e-mail address and that it's in violation of a federal law that restricts unsolicited advertisements. Many people are so intimidated by the severity of the language in the letter that they pay the bogus invoice without questioning it.

A paper shark called me one day when I was feeling particularly down about something and I mused how the sharks were circling when I felt wounded. This gave me new determination to rise above the difficult circumstances I was facing. I saw the shark as a metaphor for danger: I was 'at sea' and at risk of being swallowed up, consumed by the predators of my own fears. To save myself, I focused on the land ahead—instead of looking at the shark—and swam for shore, headed for solid ground.

6. Be Detached

Because *you're* trying to conduct business ethically, you probably expect others to be doing the same; and, when they fall short of those expectations, you might feel disillusioned or angry. To avoid being disappointed, don't expect people to behave *exactly* the way you think they should. Proceed toward your goals with dedication, but without becoming overly attached to the outcome. Instead, transform your 'needs' into *preferences*—I don't *need* that particular person's support, but it'd be nice to have—continue to work with confidence, and you'll probably end up with what you wanted or something else just as good.

7. Accept Not Knowing

"In all your getting, get understanding," the Bible wisely advises. I've often taken this passage to heart and pursued understanding to the point of obsession. I now understand a situation the best I can; then at some point, I release my fierce need to know *everything* about it and learn to be comfortable with not knowing. Maybe *that's* a lesson, too: to learn how to accept a good mystery.

An additional benefit to releasing your need to know all the answers is that you turn the problem over to your unconscious mind, which works on it while you're doing something else. The answers might then 'magically' come to you during a dream or a meditation, a coffee break, or a walk.

Also, accept that things may not *seem* to have changed, at least not on the surface. In the case of the literary agent mentioned above, Lilly heard that Joanne had left quite a few disgruntled writers behind her in her wake. If enough people object to Joanne's treatment of them, it may catch her attention, and perhaps some day she'll realize that it's best to conduct business with greater sensitivity and in a more timely fashion.

8. Let It Go

Let people's karma deal with them or, stated in modern terms, "What goes around comes around." Or you might prefer the Chinese proverb that cautions, "Let him who seeks revenge dig two graves."

Remember that there are many sources of success. Every time

I think of one particular business transaction as the *only* key to my success, I tend to get angry at the situation or angry at the person who I feel is 'responsible' if it doesn't turn out the way I wanted it to. Don't give one person or circumstance all the power over your success. A single situation or event is not your *only* opportunity for success.

There are many entrances into a building; through the front door, side door, back door, service entrance, window, garage, loading dock, skylight. And, in the unlikely event that a building is totally imprenetrable, there are *other* buildings in the city.

Lilly, the writer mentioned earlier, proved this to herself recently. When the agent finally returned her manuscript, Lilly sold it herself to an outstanding smaller publisher who wants her to write a series of books on the subject. It turns out that the agent had freed her for even greater success.

Accept the Invitation: RSVP

Consider the unethical behavior of others as an invitation for you to look at the way *you* conduct business.

Conduct Business Consciously

To conduct business consciously, whether you are the employer or the employed, means to know 'right' (what's most life-affirming) from 'wrong' (what's obtained at the expense of others or to their detriment). Conducting business consciously means to be fully present, not preoccupied, when dealing with people. It means to respect them by returning telephone calls in a timely fashion, meeting your deadlines, keeping your appointments, doing the things you say you're going to do, and living up to the ideals in your mission statement. It means to consider how your actions, attitudes, choices, and decisions affect others, and to act for the greatest good of all involved.

Take Time to Have a Conscience

Conducting business consciously also means to slow down and take some time to listen to your inner guidance. An interesting strategy used in gambling casinos is to keep things going at such a fevered pace that people don't have time to think or get in touch with their intuition or their good sense. You put yourself in similar jeopardy when you rush frantically from appointment to appointment, activity to activity, item to item, barely stopping to catch your breath.

Instead, take some time throughout the day to think about how you've been handling things at work. This might be during a coffee break, an appointment with yourself, a planned meditation, or 'found time.'

Many articles have been written about *activities* that you can do during found time—that unexpected free time here and there while you're on hold on the telephone, waiting in line, or between appointments. Instead of filling every moment with activity, use the time to reflect on how you're doing. This might be in the form of a question to yourself: "Did I handle a particular situation in the best way?" If you could have handled something more wisely, take some time to correct what you did or figure out how to handle it differently the next time. Consider the wise advice of the Roman poet Ovid: "Take a rest. A field that has rested yields a beautiful crop."

And This Is *20/20*!

Dr. Price Pritchett, author of *The Ethics of Excellence*, suggests that you take the following test when you want to check your ethics:

If what you're thinking about doing made the evening news in your hometown, how would you look? Would you be pleased to see your story on page one of the local paper?

Would you mind having your actions analyzed on '20/20'? . . . Would you care if your children knew about it? Or your parents? . . . If the threat of exposure to public scrutiny makes you squirm . . . pay attention. You're playing with something that could tarnish a reputation—yours and the organization's.

Did you work consciously today? Would the Better Business Bureau or the people who investigate business transgressions give you a seal of approval? Think about how your action (or inaction) has affected others. Take time to have a conscience and *you* won't be numbered among those who are ethically impaired— or simply so busy that they're 'missing in action.'

■

"Forgiving is not forgetting, it's letting go of the hurt."   *Mary McLeod Bethune*

■

"If someone throws salt at you, you will receive no harm unless you have sore places."   *Latin proverb*

■

"The highest form of wisdom is kindness."

The Talmud

■

"Honest differences are often a healthy sign of progress."   *Mahatma Gandhi*

■

"People are lonely because they build walls instead of bridges."   *Joseph Fort Newton*

■

"Lord, when we are wrong, make us willing to change. And when we are right, make us easy to live with."   *Peter Marshall*

■

"No one can make you feel inferior without your consent."   *Eleanor Roosevelt,* This Is My Story

■

"The saying 'Don't worry' can be improved immeasurably if you add the word *others*."

Author Unknown

■

"When you know better, you do better."

Maya Angelou

■

"He who cannot forgive breaks the bridge over which he himself must pass."   *Francis Bradley*

■

"Do I want to be right—or do I want peace?"

Marianne Williamson

■

Chapter 13

Competition
or Cooperation?

THE OTHER GUY BLINKED, a book about Pepsi and
Coca-Cola's rivalry for the greatest market share, exemplifies a
philosophy to which many businesspeople have subscribed: if we
relax for even a second and let down our guard, it's all over.
Readers are informed, "He who hesitates is lunch."

Wouldn't you frankly rather *do* lunch than *be* lunch? A
healthy get-it-done attitude is admirable, but there seems to be
something frantic or desperate in the message that we can't even
blink or we'll lose. What a stressful way to do business!

Many people today, however, are beginning to focus on values
and ethics, to encourage teamwork, and to demonstrate greater
social awareness. Cooperation is a tool and a by-product of this
emerging consciousness.

Rungs on a Ladder

Competition is built on a hierarchy of superiors and subordinates
—only one person or one company per rung on the corporate
ladder—and is based on a belief in scarcity; seize the territory

or the greater market share before someone else 'beats' you to it, try to control circumstances rather than establish connections, exploit or be exploited, and value 'subordinates' mainly for their output. In a competitive system, for someone to win, someone must lose—a practice that obscures the truth of our spiritual oneness.

Life in the Aquarium

Competition brings to mind a breed of fish, the Bettas, sometimes known as Siamese Fighting Fish. The males are so territorial that they have to be isolated from the other males in the tank. A male Betta is so combative, in fact, that it will even fight its own reflection in the glass.

We do a similar thing in the workplace if we exploit or manipulate each other, bad-mouth others, or use questionable methods to get ahead. If each of us is an individualized expression of the one Spirit—or as Marianne Williamson says, "There's only one of us here"—we're essentially fighting ourselves if we compete with each other.

Cooperation and the Spiritual Life

Cooperation is built on the principles of unity, interrelationship, and the potential for everyone to succeed without defeating or depleting someone else. In a cooperative system, people are valued because they're inherently worthy. From a spiritual perspective if we want to succeed—with integrity and a clear conscience—we must align ourselves with these principles and cooperate with the universe to bring about our highest good.

And because there's only one Energy operating in the universe, what we believe to be true for others, we must also believe, on some level, is true for ourselves. If we believe that it's possible for someone else to lose in business, for example, we automatically believe that it's possible for us to lose, too. This unconscious belief can create a fear of loss that perpetuates even more competitive behavior.

"But, people *can* lose in business. Companies have gone bankrupt. That's a fact."

That may be true on one level, but remember, fortunes can come and go and come again. Circumstances always change. Spirit's availability to you is the only constant. Each of us has an inner surplus of creativity and energy, and is capable of rising above temporary conditions. It's good, then, to look beyond circumstances, to expect the best for everyone, and to support people in their quest for success.

If we are all composed of the same Energy and, in this sense, are of one Mind, when we think of business as a contest or a war, with winners and losers, we're ultimately fighting ourselves. We're also affirming scarcity for ourselves and, ultimately, may be sabotaging our success. We might 'win' a sale or a contract, but lose in the long run because our internalized negative beliefs can erode our lives in other ways. Likewise if we work with integrity and know the truth for everyone—infinite supply and success—we affirm this for ourselves.

"But doesn't competition 'keep us on our toes'?"

Yes, it can encourage us to produce quality goods and keep our customers happy and keep them coming back, but so does living according to spiritual values. We can obtain that extra market share by competing for it or simply by enjoying our work and excelling at what we do. The question is: which approach allows us, and the people with whom we do business, to get a good night's sleep?

Celebrate Process and Involvement

Carol Record, a Unity minister in Grapevine, Texas, reminds us that:

> You're not a 'winner' if you have something that someone else doesn't have, nor are you a worthy person because of it. You're already worthy because you're a child of God, because you were born. So stop focusing on the end result and realize that you bring into any experience your self-worth as a complete, spiritual individual. When you do, you'll be free to participate fully in life.

She adds that, "Successful athletes don't focus on their scores. Many have said, "The minute I looked at the scoreboard, I wasn't living up to who I was." If they look at the scoreboard for even a second they lose the excellence of who they are. Instead they involve themselves completely in their event and they're totally present in the moment."

How to Build a Cooperative Consciousness

Many of us who've been raised in a competitive society may want to help create a more positive mindset. Here are 10 ideas:

1. Join a business or professional association whose members meet regularly to network and support each other.
2. Explore new management styles that foster cooperation.
3. Encourage participation. If you're the boss, have your employees attend brainstorming sessions, share profits, or participate in decisions that affect the whole group. If you're an employee, explore ways that these suggestions might be implemented.

4. Notice which of your beliefs are competitive and which are cooperative. If co-workers get promotions or raises, do you resent them or try to outdo them or undermine them—or do you congratulate them, knowing that your turn will come too?

5. Notice if the words you use encourage competition or cooperation. Do you 'beat' the 'competition' or 'close the deal'? Do you have 'superiors' and 'subordinates' or 'team members'?

6. Be aware of the ways that beliefs in lack and limitation are encouraged in the marketplace. Fear of loss is a technique that's often used to get us to buy products. "Buy now! You snooze, you lose." "This offer will never be repeated." "Only two left!" There are always opportunities to get what you want—or something better. So think of your needs as already having been met and live each day with confidence.

7. Team up with other organizations to achieve common goals. For example, the four major television networks, normally fierce competitors, simultaneously broadcasted a program to combat drug abuse. To explore mutually beneficial business combinations for yourself and your company, make a list of businesses and organizations, then think of innovative ways you might work together.

8. Use your energy constructively. Carol Record points out that, "When you oppose people, you oppose their very dreams and ideals. By trying to stop them, you stop yourself. If you feel competitive because someone has something you want, use that twinge of envy as an opportunity to re-evaluate what you want. Then dream your own dream and set your own goals, and all the power of the universe will support you."

9. Clarify your company—or your department's—vision. "Agree on a mission statement and meet regularly to dis-

cuss your progress," suggests Peter Turla, president of the National Management Institute. "When people share common goals, they set aside prejudices and pettiness, they work together, and they create cooperative, often permanent, bonds with each other."

10. Consider Buckminster Fuller's words. We're not going to be able to operate our spaceship earth successfully, nor for much longer, unless we see it as a whole spaceship and our fate common. It has to be everybody or nobody.

Heaven or Hell?

Cavett Robert, professional speaker and founder of The National Speakers Association, used to tell the story of a heaven and hell that were virtually identical with plenty of food for everyone. The only difference was that all the forks in both places had handles that were too long for people to be able to reach their mouths to feed themselves. The desperate inhabitants of hell panicked at the prospect of starving throughout eternity. The happier inhabitants of heaven, on the other hand, simply used the utensils differently. Instead of trying to feed themselves, they fed each other. And everyone was nourished.

Heaven and hell may indeed be identical places, defined only by a difference in attitudes and actions. Likewise the workplace may be virtually the same for each of us, with similar opportunities for us to be prosperous and successful. In business there's enough good for everyone—or not—determined by our attitudes and actions, by the way we compete—or cooperate.

■

"Separate reeds are weak and easily broken; but bound together they are strong and hard to tear apart."

The Midrash

■

"Our business in life is not to get ahead of other people, but to get ahead of ourselves."

Maltbie D. Babcock

■

"Each object in the world is not merely itself but involves every other object, and in fact is every other object."

Hindu Sutra

■

"Life isn't a race. It's a relay."

Dick Gregory

■

"You can't hold a man down without staying down with him."

Booker T. Washington

■

Chapter 14

How to Keep Your Professional Life Intact When Your Personal Life Seems to Be Falling Apart

I HAVE GOOD days and I have growing days. And then, sometimes I have good growing days,'' someone once told me. Most of us know what he means.

How can we conduct business as usual when we're having one of those excruciatingly difficult, 'growing' days—or months or years—when everything seems to be falling apart, when we're experiencing something really soul-wrenching, such as the death of a loved one or the breakup of a valued relationship.

At one time I experienced three major, unsettling events in a short period of time: a good friend died suddenly under suspect circumstances, a second friend drowned, and my two brothers became involved in a war overseas.

I expected to have some stress regarding these events, but my occasional sudden tears, difficulty concentrating, and short attention span surprised me. And in spite of my intense, varied feelings, the business world continued to make its demands with the usual deadlines, telephone calls, mailings, and meetings. I'd been given a great opportunity to test my inner strength as I endeavored to keep my business on a positive course.

18 Ways to Stay on Top of Things

We're usually allowed a week or two off work to grieve for some-one we've lost and less time than that, if any time at all, to get our lives back on track after some other personal crisis. Grief and similar emotions, however, are often longer and stronger than sympathy. Bosses, colleagues, customers, and co-workers may expect us to just 'snap out of it' and get back to work sooner than we feel ready.

We walk a fine line between dealing honestly with our feelings and not giving power to the difficult situation at hand. We have to address our feelings and take care of ourselves so we can emerge from the fray intact—personally, spiritually, and profes-sionally. Here are some ideas I've found helpful:

1. Keep connected to your lifeline. During difficult times, some people withdraw from their support systems when they need them the most. So keep in touch, even if only over the telephone, with friends, family, and people at your place of worship.

2. Tell someone you trust at work what's going on. Allow plenty of time to talk. Share your thoughts and feelings and, if appropriate, invite the other person's perspective.

3. Look for the inherent lessons in difficult situations. It's often during trying times that you can learn the fastest and the most about your life.

4. Forget being angry at God. If you believe that "the King-dom of Heaven is within"—within every experience and every constructive feeling and positive impulse you have—then getting angry at God may only be a form of turning against yourself and sabotaging your own resilience. In-stead, acknowledge that this Spirit for good is within you, and let It work through you as you seek to understand dis-turbing events.

5. Cash in on favors. It's okay to ask for help, especially during difficult times.
6. Stick to routines. Following a routine can give you some sense of security, even if you're only working at half speed.
7. Work on high-payoff items for a sense of progress. If you have loose ends in your personal life, it's especially good to have some professional wins, so complete things. If you have an unfinished project, give yourself a deadline and time to work on it every day.
8. Maximize your times of highest energy. If your most productive time is in the morning, for example, consider coming to work earlier and leaving earlier. Avoid listening to the morning news and the late-night news. This increases your chances of being more productive at work and getting a better night's sleep.
9. Schedule realistically. Leave some time open between activities. Cancel or postpone appointments, if possible, to conserve your energy. Delegate when appropriate. This will give you some breathing room.
10. Renegotiate deadlines if it looks like you might miss one. This gives others time to adjust to changes in plans, buys you more time, and preserves your credibility. Deadlines may seem trivial compared to a personal crisis, but missing them can have serious consequences in business. A deadline can help keep you steady and on course.
11. Take shorter, more frequent breaks. This way you protect your valuable energy and increase your chances of dealing more effectively with work. If you meditate, don't try to solve problems at that time. Simply use the time to rest and to return to work refreshed.
12. Exercise regularly, health permitting. Or at least do some daily stretching exercises. This way you'll better control your stress and keep yourself and your spirits in shape.
13. Remind yourself that you're the one having the 'good grow-

ing day,' not necessarily your customers. Your success at work may depend on your handling situations and transactions in your usual positive, constructive way. Remember, too, that other people may be dealing with their own emotional challenges, so keep their difficult behavior in perspective.

14. Join a support group or get counseling. Talking about your situations with others who understand can help you deal with your feelings and gain valuable insights.

15. Take action. Form your own support group or donate money, time, or talent to worthy causes. Use your insights to encourage and uplift others who might be going through similar experiences.

16. "Be in the world, not of the world." Stay centered by knowing that circumstances come and go, and that the only constant is Spirit's availability to you, waiting for you to use it.

17. Realize that others may have their own unconscious agendas for their personal growth. You may not always know all the items on those agendas. It may even be an item on your agenda to release them so they can follow their own paths to their greater good.

18. Expect things to be different. Life without a particular friend, relationship, or loved one will be different—and different isn't necessarily 'bad.' It's just *different*. Now you have a new life to pioneer. Make it an adventure.

Turn toward the Light

Be gentle with yourself while you're growing through difficult experiences. At some time or other most of us have cared for growing things, maybe taken care of a garden, fed and sheltered baby animals, or loved and nurtured children. So nurture *yourself* too as you learn, unfold, and evolve.

Turn toward the Light, toward humor, friends, good nutrition, rest, and whatever else supports you in positive, healthy ways. Allow yourself time to let go, relax, and recover. As you strive to handle personal crises more effectively while keeping your professional life on course, you might consider seeking the spiritual strength to handle whatever happens. You might want to pray as Sister Gyana Mata prayed: ''Lord, change no circumstance in my life. Change me.''

■

". . . as we grow keener in our understanding of life, we become aware that 'clinging' to anything can cause us to suffer."

The Great Religions by Which Men Live (Buddhism)

■

"Anyone who has never been disappointed has set his sights too low."

Robert Schuller

■

"Friendship is always a sweet responsibility, never an opportunity."

Kahlil Gibran

■

"As far as mind extends, so far extends heaven."

The Upanishads

■

Chapter 15

Resurrected!
*There Is No Death,
Only Transformation*

Sixty-one thousand tennis shoes spill into the ocean, a superconductor supercollider project is scrapped, a newspaper tabloid destroys a company's chance of future business with a client, a manuscript is returned, and a wildflower is mowed down along the side of the road. What do these events have in common? They each represent an ending of sorts—and they each represent the Law of Resurrection in action.

Expect Glory

To be resurrected means to overcome death and return to life. This return to life is a spiritual imperative, an ongoing, eternal impulse that cannot be stopped. And, likewise, there is no death of anything—companies, ideas, or abundance; there is only transformation. So, if you want to make progress in your life, it's essential to look beyond the 'grave'—the temporary resting-place of your fears, your expectations, and your belief in limitation—and look to the glory that is to follow.

If you try to resist the eternal flow of Energy by believing in death, thinking negatively, and fighting unpleasant circumstances —"unpleasant" because they haven't met your expectations— you entomb the Energy and risk causing yourself grief, stress, and health problems. To 'go with the flow,' see the circumstances in your life in a spiritual light. Instead of looking *at* them, look *through* them to the underlying, unifying truth. This truth is the 'implicate order,' which Hindus call "Brahma," Buddhists call the "Tao," Christians call "God," physicists call the "unified field," and physicist David Bohm calls "spirit." Bohm goes on to say that ". . . when a [subatomic] particle appears to be destroyed, it is not lost. It is merely enfolded back into the deeper order from which it sprang."

Likewise, when a job or a business venture appears to be lost, the creative energy behind it is simply absorbed back into the deeper order to ready itself for rebirth.

One Idea, Many Forms

A wonderful example of the continuing rebirth of an idea is the way writers can turn an idea into many forms, even one that has been returned by a publisher. Writers can:

1. turn their short stories into poems or novels and their novels or poems into short stories
2. make the information in their articles into checklists to be used by themselves or used as sidebars in other people's articles
3. sell reprints—'second serial rights'—of their published articles
4. sell foreign rights to their work
5. sell rewrites of reprints and reprints of rewrites
6. slant an idea to a particular age group, region, or season and thereby develop it into several articles

7. turn their how-to books into audio-cassette programs or videos
8. parlay their books or articles into seminars and lectures
9. use their public presentations as the basis of books and articles
10. sell film rights to their work
11. ask for a 'kill fee' if they've been assigned to write an article, which the editor then decides not to use. A kill fee is about 25 percent of what a writer would have been paid if the piece had been published

If writers insist that a certain piece of writing take a particular form—"it *has* to be a screenplay or *nothing*!"—they become unreceptive to the other forms the idea could take. And if they entomb their creative energy this way, it could manifest in less constructive ways such as anger, depression, frustration, poor health, or writer's block.

Likewise an idea that you have at work can take many forms. If a plan or a project appears to be stalled or seems to have run into a dead end, give it some more thought. Look for other ways it might express itself. Do some more research, ask for people's input, pray about it, meditate on it. Explore the possibilities and let it show you the way. Let it evolve and find its own form.

Creativity Is Mushrooming

To the great disappointment of many people, the superconducting supercollider project was scrapped in Waxahachie, Texas. Five miles of dark, damp tunnels 200 feet underground sat idle and unused where scientists had once dreamed of smashing atoms.

The abandonment of the project in 1993 gave rise to many creative ideas. An investor from Fort Worth stepped forward and asked to use the tunnel for an agricultural venture. The tunnel, carved from rock similar to limestone and sealed with concrete, maintains a steady temperature of 70° and is a perfect environment for growing mushrooms. Someone else wanted to use it for a linear accelerator that could become the basis for a cancer therapy center. And still someone else suggested that the accelerator be used to manufacture radioactive isotopes for use in diagnostic medicines. What was finally done? The government gave the land and the equipment to the public schools.

Buildings Evolve

A meat-packing plant, with elaborate refrigeration and ventilation systems, went out of business in Boulder, Colorado, and later became the perfect site for a tofu factory. Many other abandoned buildings across the country have also been refurbished, brought up to code, rezoned when necessary, and converted into recreation centers, day-care centers, senior centers, and pet hotels.

Ideas Evolve

Look around you. Everything you see started as a thought: the computer you use, the books you read, the airplane you take on vacations or business trips. Even you and your co-workers started as an idea in the minds of a couple of people.

The first humans had a need to communicate with each other, which led to a few drawings on the wall of a cave, then evolved into stone tablets, scrolls, paper and pencils and pens, printing presses, manual typewriters, electric typewriters, computers, and—who knows where it will lead?

Flight began as a thought in the Wright brothers' minds, then became a goal, then a history-making achievement. Improvements were made on the plane and new aircraft were invented and produced: small one-pilot planes, helium balloons, pontoon planes, jet liners, jet fighters, rockets, unmanned space probes, moon rockets, moon landings, space shuttles, space stations and—who knows where it'll lead: maybe to the invention of warp drives, the exploration of wormholes, and travel to distant galaxies and beyond.

Likewise, you cannot think a thought in isolation. A thought that you have today is not the beginning and the end of that idea. Your thoughts came from somewhere and are going somewhere; they're passing through you and evolving. Your job, career, business or profession, your relationships, your life—everything is in a state of motion and progress. Or as the sign said on the side of a bus in San Francisco: **"Something's moving."—Albert Einstein.**

Recipes Evolve

I'm not a great cook usually. I've even seen a *dog* spit out something that I made (pumpkin bread). And you know that dogs will eat almost *anything*. So I'm a lousy cook, but surprise, surprise! I won first prize in a cooking contest! I had so many 'failures' that I actually invented something original, tasty and —according to the judges—worthy of first prize in the 'Main Dish' category of a cooking contest. Now I sometimes think to myself, "Help me 'fail' faster so I can succeed sooner. Each 'failure' moves me closer to what I want or moves me in delightful new directions."

I'm in good company. I've heard that Alexander Graham Bell was trying to invent a hearing aid when he invented the telephone instead—by mistake.

Disaster Evolves into Opportunity

In 1990, a container ship carrying a load of tennis shoes being transported from Korea to the United States was hit by a storm. Five of the containers, each as large as a boxcar, broke loose and spilled 61,000 tennis shoes into the ocean. The shoes were caught in various ocean currents and floated to far-reaching destinations: all the way up the California coastline, as far north as British Columbia, and as far west as Hawaii. The disaster, which the company wrote off as a business loss at tax time, became someone else's opportunity. Oceanographers were given the chance to study the drift of ocean currents by how far the shoes were carried and where they washed ashore.

The Magic of Release

What's the difference between giving up and letting go? Be careful how you answer. Your success could depend on it.

'Giving up' means to resign yourself to circumstances, to feel defeated by them, and to quit working on the dream or the goal. 'Letting go,' on the other hand, means to release your expectations for a particular outcome and therefore to free your creative energy to hunt for answers and solutions. When you do this, you feel lighter and enlightened. You continue working toward your goal, but you work with confidence and you release the exact form that success will take—even release how soon it gets done. The universe may have a different schedule than you.

Dr. Hans Selye, an expert on stress management, describes an interesting phenomenon that he calls the 'Alarm/Resistance Phenomenon.' Simply put, when faced with something alarming, people often resist it as long as they can, then finally let go. Then, *after* letting go, they experience their first symptoms of stress. Maybe you've heard people say that they're calm during emergencies, but break down *after* the crisis. They contain the tension long enough to do what needs to be done; then, when the crisis is over, they stop resisting—sometimes at the expense of their health or sense of well-being.

I've noticed something similar to this build-up of tension and subsequent release of energy operating in life, *but in a more positive way*. When I think that I absolutely *must* have something, it eludes me. It's only when I 'bottom out,' exhaust myself trying to make something happen, and grow too tired to hold on, that things begin to happen as if by magic. It's as if there's a tremendous build-up of energy that I can contain just so long, then can't control any more. And only when I release it does it burst forth into the world and go searching to bring back what I want.

At one time, for example, I tried everything I could think of to get published, then finally declared that I was a writer, published or not. I even stopped sending my work out. I'd released my *need* to be published and instead started writing a personal newsletter, which I just sent to friends. Three months later an editor at *Success* magazine asked me to write an article for the magazine. This led to a lucrative five-year relationship with the magazine, four book contracts, and a best-seller. Now I've learned that if I'm going to release my need sooner or later for things to be a certain way, why not *sooner*?

Still in Circulation

After I 'lost' the $8000 on the bad investment with the oil tycoon mentioned in Chapter 12, I finally concluded that the money hadn't been lost at all. It's still in circulation and will stay in circulation until the end of time—or until the end of currency as we know it. I'd love to be able to trace the money from my bank account to the account of the ethically impaired man who relieved me of it to wherever it went from there—maybe to pay his doctor's bills or pay the employees at the wheelchair company —he'd had some sort of misfortune that had left him wheelchair-bound. Or maybe my money—no, not *my* money, just the $8000 —has been reinvested in a school district, used as a down payment on a family's first home, or converted into another currency and is now being used in Europe, Africa, or Asia. Whatever the case, may it continue to be resurrected into countless forms and multiply!

Raise Your Consciousness from the Dead

The 'dead' in this case refers to the gloom and doom that we all encounter occasionally. And the 'resurrection' refers to the progress, or the evolution, of our consciousness. Limitation is simply a human invention, circumstances are temporary, all barriers fall away eventually, and the human spirit bursts forth and rises every time. It is Spirit's nature to grow, prosper, and evolve. And, since you are one with this Spirit, it's also *your* nature to grow, prosper, and evolve.

Have you ever experienced the 'fight or flight' phenomenon, that sudden rush of adrenaline you feel when you're in danger? Say 'hello' to life asserting itself. Or maybe you've had a peak experience, an oceanic feeling of being one with everything. Again, say 'hello' to life. Nothing can stop this impulse for long, nothing can stop the resurrection of your creativity, your ideals, your compassion, the rising again of your spirit out of the tomb of despair, doubt, fear, and failure. The stone *will* roll away.

Gaining through Loss

Many of us go to work to make money, hopefully doing something we love that contributes something of value to others. In doing so, we spend most of our time earning our paychecks, achieving our goals, and acquiring accounts, clients, or prestige. We're geared up to 'get' and gain; but if we're in the workplace long enough, it's likely we'll encounter a loss of some kind, such as a scandal, a hostile takeover, a bad investment, a less-than-complimentary performance review, a stock market correction, or the loss of a valued objective.

We need to learn from these events or we shall be destined to keep reliving them. In our company it sometimes takes a while to understand what we've gained from our losses, but we do, eventually. In one case, one of our promoters went bankrupt.

We lost all future business with him but gained the clients he'd had who now do business directly with us.

In another case, we lost a new national client because we gave an interview to a reporter for a newspaper tabloid. She wanted our ideas for a short article on how to meet deadlines. "Nothing scandalous there," we thought; "what could possibly go wrong?" So we granted her the interview.

Well, the tabloid's facts-verification department called our client to confirm that we were who we said we were but didn't explain that one of their writers was simply quoting us in an article on how to meet deadlines. Our client, probably not wanting to be associated with a company who they thought was affiliated with the tabloids, canceled an upcoming class—the first class they had ever scheduled with us. They claimed that they didn't have the budget for the class—even though they were a Fortune 500 company. Further, they didn't know when their budget would allow them to schedule such a class! We tried to explain the situation to the client, then complained to the writer who apologized for mishandling the article. But there was little else we could do other than vow never again to grant such an interview.

The *good* news is that about 18 million people read the article, which led to dozens of radio interviews and increased book sales—but at the time that was little consolation. The experience with the tabloid had been one of those terribly embarrassing situations that left us questioning our judgment and wondering why the person verifying the facts didn't check out the story of the woman who gave birth to Big Foot's baby, a common story that appears regularly in the tabloids!

The temporary setback with the tabloid, however, as painful as it was, didn't put us out of business. One corporate client, in fact, just scheduled my associate and me to teach 36 trainings—each—in one year alone, for a total of 72 trainings!

A Future Freed Up

When we have a 'loss' at our company, as in the case of the tabloid fiasco, it gives us extra time to cultivate more business, pursue writing projects, attend conventions, network, and let our creative energy flow into other channels.

To deny a loss or dwell on it is to multiply it. Instead, let it sink in and feel the emotions—pain, anger, frustration, discomfort, etc. Relate to it from a spiritual perspective and transform it. Resolve your emotions in order to move through them and then move on, your creativity resurrected, your enthusaism restored.

Roots and Flowers

In Texas, where I live now, the most beautiful wildflowers grow along the country roads in the spring. One afternoon as I was driving home from town I noticed someone from a road crew mowing down the primroses along one stretch of road. I was disturbed by it until I remembered that even though the flowers were gone, the roots were still intact and, with each mowing, the ripe seeds were scattered even further. The wildflowers have been growing there as long as I can remember, and every year there are more flowers than the year before—thick carpets of flowers, in some places as far as the eye can see.

Has something in business or at work that you've been 'growing,' been mowed down or rejected? Remember that the root—your inner creativity and the impulse to make progress—is still intact, ready to rise and bloom again.

"What the caterpillar calls the end of the world, the master calls a butterfly."

Richard Bach

"If there is a good and wise God, then there also exists a progress of humanity toward perfection."

Plato

"For now we see through a glass, darkly; but then face to face."

Paul, 1 Corinthians 13:12

"Since each soul is some part of the Whole, it is impossible that any soul can be lost."

Ernest Holmes, The Science of Mind

"After the final 'no,' there comes a 'yes,' and on that 'yes' the future world depends."

Wallace Stevens

Chapter 16

Negotiating and Spirit
*How to Get What You Want
with the Cooperation of Others
So that Everyone Wins*

BY ITS very nature business can get complicated. Transactions involve people, products, prices, and profits. And exchanges of ideas, goods, and services. If everyone had the same needs, business might be simple. But people usually have different goals, budgets, and time frames. And when the needs of one person conflict with the needs of another, it's necessary to negotiate.

Many people resist negotiating, however, because they have negative interpretations of the word. For them *negotiate* means to argue, dicker, haggle, wrangle—not flattering activities for the spiritually inclined. To some people, negotiating suggests pettiness or aggressiveness, and for others it gives rise to doubts: Am I being too materialistic? Do I deserve to get a deal or obtain a coveted contract? Will I be taking advantage of people if I ask for a discount? Will they try to take advantage of me?

More positive interpretations of the word *negotiate* include: bargain, barter, hurdle, compromise, adjust, agree, and arrange. But negotiation goes deeper than all the subjective definitions.

Negotiating is as natural as breathing. And you've been doing it all your life.

1. As a baby, you 'asked' for what you wanted by crying or smiling at the adults. In exchange for getting what you wanted, you took your nap or entertained them with delightful antics.
2. As a child you negotiated who got to sit by the window on family trips, your allowance, or what chores you were going to do.
3. As a teenager you negotiated how late you could stay out at night or how long you could have the car.
4. As an adult you've asked for time off, bought large-ticket items, asked to have deadlines extended, and discussed with others where to go for dinner or what to do for entertainment.

Whenever you influence, persuade, bargain, or convince someone, you engage in some form of negotiation. Since you've been negotiating your entire life and will continue to do so, it makes sense to understand the process and be good at it. Negotiating from a spiritual perspective means to get what you want with the cooperation of others so that everyone wins.

For some people, though, negotiation can be a form of competition. For others, it's a way to prove their intellectual superiority, and for still others it's a test of their own self-worth. In these cases, power and accomplishment are obtained at the expense of others. This addresses a common fear that many businesspeople have: if I become more spiritual, will the less spiritually inclined try to run me over, chew me up, and spit me out?

One way to guard against being used is to be a savvy negotiator and to realize that you can be assertive and spiritual at the same time. Only when we affirm and support each other can we begin to find mutually beneficial ways to work together.

Fear—or Friend—of the Unknown

What makes negotiating scary for a lot of us? Probaby the fear of the unknown.

1. We're unfamiliar with the techniques that we can use in negotiations.
2. We don't know what techniques others might use to gain the upper hand.
3. Sellers don't know the top price that buyers will pay, and buyers don't know the lowest price that sellers will accept. This can lead to fancy maneuvering, sophisticated tactics, and game-playing.
4. We're concerned that we might be taken advantage of, our sense of self-worth challenged, or our confidence undermined.

When we fear the unknown, we're coming from a position of apprehension, dread, and worry. We imagine the worst possible outcome. But when we make friends with the unknown, we acknowledge that it's also a place of infinite possibilities where everyone can be satisfied.

When we approach negotiations with this frame of mind, we increase the chances of achieving a successful outcome in which the buyer receives a fair price and the seller makes a reasonable profit, or everyone agrees to the terms of a contract and the parties are likely to do business with each other again. But perhaps most important, a successful negotiation leaves people's self-esteem intact. This is accomplished when our common needs are acknowledged, addressed, and satisfied.

Meet a Need

When you meet other people's needs, you increase the chances of having your own needs met. Most of us want to:

- solve problems
- make money
- get ahead socially, financially, and professionally
- do a good job
- enjoy life
- feel good about ourselves
- be distinct, special, and outstanding
- feel confident, smart, and worthy
- save time
- feel important and respected

In each of the following cases, notice the human needs that are either met or disregarded. The item referred to in each scenario is a color copier, but you can substitute any item you might consider purchasing, such as furniture, a car, office equipment, an appliance, or a magazine subscription.

I Win / You Lose

In this scenario you refuse to buy an item, say a color photocopier, from an aggressive salesperson. You keep saying "no" and finally throw the person out of the office, slam down the telephone, or storm out of the store. You've won—you got rid of an unpleasant person and saved your money—but you've also lost your peace of mind temporarily. And the salesperson has clearly lost the sale and maybe his or her dignity.

I Lose / You Win

Here, you buy a color copier that you didn't want because the salesperson was pushy and you were manipulated into buying an item you didn't need or which was beyond your budget. The salesperson won by making a sale that was obtained by disrespecting and manipulating you. And you've spent money on an item you didn't really want and, maybe, lost some self-esteem by not having been assertive enough.

I Lose / You Lose

In this case you cave in to sales pressure and say, "I can't afford your best copier . . . but, well, okay . . . I'll buy your least expensive one." Now you've got buyer's remorse and you're unhappy with yourself, with the salesperson, and with what might be an inferior machine. The salesperson gets a small commission but loses future sales.

I Win / You Win

In this situation both parties reach a satisfactory agreement in which both gain something they consider valuable and neither gives up anything significant. Suppose that you want to buy a color copier in the near future, but you're just window shopping today. Your goals are to educate yourself as to what's available and to save money when you do buy a copier. And the salesperson's goal is to sell you a top-of-the-line, expensive machine.

If you're going to want a copier some time, but not today, you're in a perfect position to negotiate. Because you're not in a hurry to buy one, you can negotiate from a comfortable position of power.

The salesperson wants to make a sale today and might be willing to take some extra time to explain the various features of several machines and suggest which models would best fit your budget. He or she might also be open to giving you a good deal, arranging to service the machine at a special price, letting you have supplies at a discount, and scheduling a delivery time that's convenient for you. But for this to happen you have to—ask.

8 Steps for Planning a Succesful Negotiation

Before you negotiate anything, it's smart to do some planning in advance. The following guidelines apply to almost any situation—personal or professional.

1. Be very clear about the goal or the results you want.
2. Review the human needs listed earlier in this chapter. Be prepared to take these into account when you negotiate.
3. Determine what you're willing to give up, or pay in terms of time, money, and energy to get what you want, and at what point you'd be willing to walk away from a negotiation. Whatever you decide, keep that information to yourself until the time is right to address it.
4. Anticipate the other parties' major needs, goals, and desires as well as their *secondary* needs, goals, and desires. A major need might be for a seller to make a sale. A secondary need might be to save himself or herself time if you're not interested in buying a product or a service. Develop alternatives and contingency plans to meet those needs for people without giving up what you value.
5. Research the other parties' backgrounds and find out the amount of time or money they have available to negotiate. The more aware you are of the issues, the easier it'll be to negotiate.
6. Identify the areas in which you already agree. This gives you a basis on which to build the negotiations.
7. Be prepared to negotiate more than just money issues. You can also negotiate timing, workload, assignments, priorities, personnel, product, delivery, service, and location.
8. Before you go into a negotiation remind yourself that Spirit is in every situation and affirm your unity with it. Then visualize positive results for everyone involved. Remember, your goal is a win/win outcome.

Once you've done the necessary planning, use any or all of the following professional approaches and strategies.

11 Techniques the Professionals Use

There's almost always room to negotiate, and almost everything is negotiable. When sellers set prices, for example, they take into account what a product costs them to produce. Then they 'mark up' the price to include a profit for themselves. They usually can afford to give a little if they want to make a sale—and still make a profit. Likewise you'll want to give yourself room to negotiate so *your* customers feel that they got a good deal. Mark something up a bit and let people talk you down a bit. That way the other party feels good and you get a fair price.

1. Explore the 'Wiggle Room'

Good managers usually build extra time into deadlines to allow for the unexpected. They frequently tell people that the deadline is sooner than it really is. When I was writing my column for *Success* magazine, for example, my editor told me to get the articles to him by the 20th of each month. I usually met the deadline, but one month I had an unexpected crisis and was feeling a lot of pressure to meet the deadline. So I asked if I could have some extra time, and he said, "Sure; if you get it to me by the first, that'll be fine."

All along I'd assumed that the deadline wasn't negotiable. After that, I usually sent my articles by the 20th, but I felt more relaxed if I needed an extra day or two.

First there's the announced deadline, which often has a time cushion built into it; then there's the 'drop dead date.' If you don't have something in by the drop-dead date, you're done for. When you negotiate deadlines or delivery schedules, find out what the drop-dead date is.

In addition to the deadlines, you can often find wiggle room in other areas as well, such as service, price, and delivery date.

This might seem like a lot of game-playing, but it's done every day in the workplace and is likely to continue. There's room to be flexible, fortunately, and so there's a greater chance of more people getting what they want.

2. Ask the Right Questions

You may be able to negotiate the price on a high-ticket item if you ask, "Will this item be on sale in the near future? Has it been on sale lately? How much did you sell it for in the past when it was on sale? Are you planning any markdowns in price? How big a markdown?" This way you get an idea of the true selling-price of an item and you're able to make a more acceptable offer. You also can ask, "If I pay cash instead of using a credit card, how much of a discount can you give me?" Or, "If I buy this, can you throw in another item as well, or throw in a second item at a discount?" Or, "Will you give me a discount if I buy both items together?"

3. Make Me an Offer

To more thoroughly understand the other parties' price ranges or goals, get them to make the first offer. If someone asks, for example, "How much do you want for that car?" a good answer would be, "Make me an offer." The person might surprise you and come up with an offer that's better than you expected.

4. The Wince

The 'Wince' is usually a natural response to someone else's offer or price quote. Variations on the Wince include a frown, a startled expression, a grimace, or a disappointed look. In some cases, the Wince is a deliberate tactic on the part of other people to make you feel uneasy and, therefore, more pliable. So be aware that the Wince could be used against you. But whether it's natural or deliberate, it often works.

If you want a deal or a discount, be sure you're talking to the person with the authority to make those decisions such as the boss, owner, or manager. He or she will probably quote a price that's higher than you expected to pay, in which case it'll be natural for you to flinch or look surprised. People generally like to please others, and if they see you do this, they may be willing to come down a bit in price.

5. Can You Do Any Better?

Then ask a powerful, but simple five-word question: "Can you do any better?" Usually they can.

Once I saw a piece of used furniture that I wanted. The asking price was $300. I asked the seller if she could do any better and she exclaimed, "One hundred and fifty dollars and that's the lowest I can go." I wrote her a check on the spot. 50 percent off was a pretty good deal. And she made a sale.

6. Refer to a Higher Authority

If you want time to think about an offer, tell the other party that you have to check with someone who has more authority than you: your manager, spouse, accountant, or head of the shipping department. The higher authority could also be your inner guidance, although you wouldn't tell the other party that you want time to meditate or pray about a situation.

This delay also adds perceived value to the deal because you've gotten the 'okay' from someone with more authority to make decisions, which lets the other parties know that you've gone the extra mile to make them happy.

7. Mention the Competition

Find out who else is selling the item you want and for what price. Then you can tell the seller something like, "I saw this somewhere else for less, but I'd rather do business with you be-

cause you're in the neighborhood. Can you do any better?"
Many people want to keep you as a customer, so this may be the
incentive they need to give you a discount. After all, wouldn't
you be willing to do that to keep someone's business?

8. Be Willing to Walk Away

If the other party's offer is unacceptable, be willing to leave.
Often the other party will reopen negotiations. I once walked
away from a negotiation for a new car. The salesperson called
me that evening at home and suggested I come in again and she'd
give me a better deal.

9. Beware of the Phony Offer

There's an unethical tactic that may be used against you, so
be on the lookout for it: the phony-offer technique. A salesperson might say, "I know you want that item, but I've got someone else who's interested in it. Unless you can pay me today the
price I'm asking, I'm going to have to sell it to the other person."
If this phony-offer technique is pulled on you, consider calling
the salesperson's bluff. Say something like, "That's a chance I'll
have to take," and be ready to walk away.

10. Use Silence Effectively

Often in negotiations you'll need to think carefully about
what's being said. Take all the time you need to do this, even in
the middle of a negotiation. If you meditate on a regular basis,
you're probably comfortable with silence. You may also find that
the quieter you are, the more the other person feels the need to
speak up to fill the silence. I discovered this when I went to buy
a mattress. I definitely planned on buying one and spent a fair
amount of time in the store considering a particular brand. But
first I wanted to look around a bit and proceeded to stroll lei-

surely through the store. The salesperson followed me around and, afraid that I might walk out and he'd lose a sale, he lowered the price every few minutes until he'd taken $100 off.

11. Be Sure You Understand Each Other

To keep communication clear, you might say something like, "To be sure I understand your thinking on this, you're saying you'd increase your order if we could deliver the product to you by the first of each month. And you want to be sure we could do that. Is that right?"

It's important that the other parties know that you want to help them meet some of their needs. You'll also want to find out how they feel as well as think. You might ask questions such as, "How do you feel about what I'm suggesting?"

When you use the 11 techniques discussed above, you'll be a more confident negotiator. But can you use them if you're an employee and your *boss* makes unfair or unrealistic demands on you?

The Boss Wins/I Win

Suppose your boss comes running in an hour before closing and asks you to redo some figures that might make you miss your dinner date. Do you stay late? If you do, you could be setting a precedent as well as turning the situation into a 'Boss wins/I lose' situation. The boss gets the work done, but also gets a resentful employee.

How can you turn this into a mutually beneficial situation? First look at what both of you want. Your boss wants the figures redone and you want to go to dinner. Then consider what can be negotiated. Do they really need to be done *tonight* after hours? By *you personally*? At *the office*?

Ask if your boss would be willing to help you reset priorities on your other assignments, have someone else do the figures or help you with your workload, or change deadlines on the tasks already assigned you. You could also negotiate *when* you'll put in those extra hours. Instead of staying late, could you come in early sometime to do the work or stay later on another night? Could you do some of the work at home or use an empty conference room where you could work undisturbed until you finish the figures? The more options you have in a situation, the more likely you'll succeed when negotiating.

What Teresa Did

Teresa negotiated a contract between Bruce, who had written a book about a scientific discovery he'd made, and a publisher, Don, who wanted to publish the book. Don ordered a large first printing of the book, but shortly after, Bruce had an emotional breakdown and couldn't promote it.

Don had overextended himself financially and, after several agonizing months, went out of business. He offered to sell the remaining stock for three dollars a book to either Bruce, who was too sick to return his calls and too broke to afford it, or to Teresa.

Teresa realized that Bruce couldn't afford the publisher's inventory, so she decided to buy it and sell it to Bruce when he regained his health and his finances improved. She knew that if she didn't buy the books, Don would sell them to a liquidation company for scrap, for which he'd be paid only .25–.50 a book. Liquidation companies, incidentally, usually make their offers over the telephone or in writing to avoid angry confrontations because they offer so little to the desperate sellers whose dreams are going down the drain.

Teresa wanted to make money but didn't want to take advantage of Don. Instead she wanted to reward his belief in Bruce's scientific discovery, on which the book was based. She also wanted to keep the lines of communication open and encourage Don to cooperate with her in the future if other business opportunities came up.

Teresa knew that she could have paid a rock-bottom price for the publisher's closeout (the .25–.50 a liquidation company would have paid), but she gave Don $1.00 a book because he'd believed in the book when no one else would. She'd be out some money initially but figured she'd either make a profit eventually, break even, or be able to declare it as a business loss on her taxes. In addition she'd maintain her relationship with Don.

Both Don and Teresa got a fair deal. Don made more money on the books by selling them to Teresa than he would have made by selling them to a liquidation house, and Teresa got the books at a discount from Don.

Teresa told me, "I feel good about the decisions I've made, and I sleep well at night."

"You Got a *Great* Deal!"

When negotiations are finished, tell the other parties that they got a great deal—which will be the case if the negotiation was done right. This makes the other people feel good and can lead to future business with them and long-lasting, positive relationships.

Negotiating is a powerful tool to get ahead in life. By understanding each other's goals and needs, you can work together to each other's mutual benefit so that each of you is happy with the outcome. You have both asked. And you have both received.

■

"Let us never negotiate out of fear. But let us never fear to negotiate."

John F. Kennedy, Inaugural Address

■

"The highest revelation is that God is in everyone."

Ralph Waldo Emerson, Journals

■

"Spiritually, there is only God; but in attaining God, we attain all that God is, God appearing in all form. Let us not seek the forms of God but seek the allness of God, and in seeking the allness of God, we shall have all the forms necessary to our own unfoldment."

Joel Goldsmith, Practicing the Presence

■

Chapter 17

Service and Sales

*23 Ways to Inspire People
to Do Business with You*

A STORY IS told of two candy-store owners—both successful, one rich. The difference is in the way each of them weighs candy. The first owner puts a pile of candy on the scale and scoops off some to get the right amount. The second, more successful, puts a little candy on the scale, then *adds* to it to get the right amount. And then he puts a little *more* on top to tip the scale in the customer's favor. He thereby tips it in his *own* favor, too: he has a happy customer who will give him repeat business.

All things being equal, which of the candy stores above would *you* patronize? And which of the following people would get your business?

- The beauty salon attendant who cuts your hair quickly— or the one who takes some time to discuss which hair style would be the most flattering for you?
- The mechanic who tells you what's wrong with your car—or the one who takes some time to be sure you understand the problem and what repairs need to be done?

- The travel agent who simply sells you a ticket—or the one who finds you the best deal?
- The person who simply sells you a service—or the one who can recommend related services that might be helpful, as well, such as the travel agent who also knows a good house-sitter, the chiropractor who knows a massage therapist, the pet-food supplier who knows a veterinarian or a dog-trainer in your area.

If you'd patronize the businesses that cheerfully give you a little more than you expected or paid for, and who treat you with respect, it makes sense to use a similar approach when you provide *your* services to others. And in doing so, both you and your customers benefit.

Your Store, Your "Church"

"Your store is your church," Marianne Williamson writes in her book *A Return to Love*. "Church, esoterically, means the gathering of souls." She then suggests that the sale of goods and services is secondary to the ultimate opportunity that you have to give people love: service, support, assistance, and respect.

What a fantastic concept! What would happen if you treated your customers and clients with reverence and, in turn, were revered by them? What if we all treated each other as we might treat each other in church or synagogue, where we tend to be on our best behavior? What if we thought of our jobs as our spiritual practice and our offices as a proving ground for our highest values? We might begin to see the workplace in an entirely different light.

Rather than thinking of your product or service simply as a way to make money, think of it in terms of how it can help others by answering their needs: the need to belong, be respected, be liked and accepted, feel safe and secure, succeed, find love and romance, and be inspired. When you meet those needs and incorporate some of the strategies discussed below into the way you do business, you'll be way ahead of the game.

23 Ways to Inspire People to Do Business with You

People earn college degrees in sales, service, and marketing. The best 'classroom' experience that I've found, however, is the world about me. You might want to ask successful businesspeople which two or three strategies they've found the most helpful. And carry a small notebook with you to record all the effective techniques that you encounter in your travels.

If you're the owner of a business or the boss, you're in a good position to implement some of the ideas below. If you work for someone else, you might want to share some of these ideas with your boss. This way you can show management that you care about the success of the company. And you play a part in that success.

1. Give free samples. Who can resist a warm, fresh-from-the-oven chocolate chip cookie, a five-minute neck rub from a massage therapist in a shopping mall, a fresh flower with a cheerful note, or an article with useful information?

2. Appeal to people's altruism. Provide your service in exchange for people bringing in canned goods for the hungry at Thanksgiving or stuffed animals for needy children at the holidays. This makes it possible for people to help others and feel good about themselves.

3. Give discounts. In my area, for example, massage therapists charge $40–$50 an hour—only one charges $35, because she wants to provide a worthwhile service to people who can't pay the higher prices. Many of the therapists need more business. The one who charges a little less has all the business she wants.

4. If you give presentations, have a stash of giveaways on hand. People love to get 'stuff.' I know a speaker to the construction industry who gives away toy trucks, another speaker who gives dollar bills to people who answer questions during his presentation, and a professor who hands out packets of cheese and crackers as prizes for the learning games they play in her classes. I've given away pencils made of compressed recycled money, bookmarkers listing my key points, "Do Not Disturb" signs for doorknobs, miniature race cars, and apple ornaments—because teachers shouldn't be the only ones who get apples.

5. Hire first-rate people to answer the telephones, and pay them well. They make a powerful impression on potential customers who call your company.

6. Make it easy for people to be your customers. Adjust your hours so they're convenient. And give people a variety of ways to reach you to place orders: e-mail, fax, mail-in orders, credit card, a toll-free telephone number.

7. If you have a 'designer' telephone number, such as 1(800) 555-CARE (2273), translate the letters into their respective numbers and put them in parentheses as shown in this example. This reduces the chance of people dialing the wrong number, which can be irritating and frustrating.

8. Consider promoting your business on the Internet. We're a global economy now, and you may want to expand your horizons.

9. If you have customers in other countries or advertise on a global scale, when you leave a telephone number for people to return your call be sure to state the date and time you called and give the entire telephone number including the country code.

10. Stress the *benefits* of a product rather than the features. Sell the fragrance, not the flower, and suggest how it can add romance to people's lives; sell the beautiful music, not the

instrument, and how it can soothe people's nerves; sell the smooth, safe ride, not the car, and how it can protect people's friends and loved ones.

11. Make satisfied customers part of your team by making it easy for them to tell others about you. Give them feedback forms, then draft your own letter of recommendation based on their comments and have them sign the letter if they agree. This way you do the work for them, you get a recommendation, and potential customers will appreciate hearing what others have to say about you and your product.

12. Give people subscriptions for magazines or newsletters to thank them for their business. This way they'll remember you at least once a month. Be sure, though, to tell the subscription department *not* to give people's names to other companies for their mailing lists.

13. Offer specials: two-for-one or buy-so-many-and-get-one-free or buy-so-many-and-get-one-at-a-reduced-price.

14. Be genuinely excited about your product. You can't light a fire with a wet match.

15. Make company literature a 'keeper' by adding information that people will want to save. Aim to educate, inform, or entertain and you'll find that you're advertising, inadvertently, as well.

16. Do something different, playful, or amusing to get attention, like delivering a singing telegram about your service or sending prospective buyers a tape or video of your product. On occasion I've sent a package of herbal tea and gourmet cookies with a manuscript along with an invitation to the editor to make a cup of tea, get comfortable, and prepare to read a good 'book.' I sold a manuscript to a publisher who received such a package and had another say that she'd enjoyed the cookies.

17. Serve people in a fair, consistent, and timely manner. If

you're particularly busy, you might want to farm out some business, create a franchise, or hire temporary help or additional employees.

18. Be willing to advertise other companies' services to help each other out. A pool and spa dealer, for example, might be able to suggest a nursery where customers could go to buy outdoor, ornamental plants.

19. Be creative. One afternoon in New York City, I looked out my second-story hotel room window. One particular van below caught my attention as it made its way through traffic. On top of the van, in bold letters, a name and telephone number were printed: **DAN'S FLORIST (212) 555-1232**. How resourceful! For just the cost of some stencils and a bit of paint, Dan was advertising his business to hundreds of thousands of people, to everyone above the first floor of every high-rise office building and hotel that he passed. He had virtually no competition.

20. Keep notes about your customers' families, hobbies, and birthdays so that when you talk with them you can mention their interests. They'll be honored that you remembered.

21. Be high profile. Participate in community service, write articles for regional newspapers and magazines, and join associations or the Chamber of Commerce.

22. Personalize your communication to create a sense of community and teamwork. Use the words *I*, *we*, *us*, and *you*, rather than general words such as *people*, *customers*, or *buyers*.

23. Hire people who genuinely *care* about the customers—or be such a person. If you can't help someone, say something like, "I'm sorry I don't know . . . let me look . . . let me ask someone . . . I'll find out . . . I'll get back to you with the information . . . I'll do some research . . . I'll ask my supervisor . . . I'll find a way to help you."

When you combine the techniques above with a reverence for people, they'll feel respected and cared for. And they'll look forward to doing business with you.

The Customer Is Always Right (?)

"Is the customer always right?" I asked a highly successful customer service representative. He smiled and answered, "The customer is not always right, but the customer is always the customer."

My patience and peace of mind were tested one day when a man called our office and asked for a refund. He'd purchased my audio-cassette album *How to Organize Yourself to Win* and complained about it: "There was so much information on it that we all had to listen to it several times to get everything we needed from it!"

I told him that's usually what people loved about the program: the fact that there was so much good, practical information in it. That's why it became a best-seller. He repeated that he wanted his money back! He sounded disgruntled—or maybe guilty? In his opinion, I'd overwhelmed him with too much information, so he felt he was 'right' to want his money back. I thought that his ethics were off—he and his friends or his co-workers had used the material for free—but I remembered that people can rationalize any behavior, and I simply refunded his money rather than argue with him.

If you're selling a large-ticket item or have a chance of doing repeat business with people, however, you might want to explore all the options available to you to save a sale or keep a customer. Maybe you could give them another product instead or a discount, or upgrade the service agreement.

When customers are happy with a company, product, or service, they tend to tell 3 people, but when they're *unhappy*, they tell at least 10 people! So do what you can to keep people happy, but maintain your self-respect in the process. Be assertive, helpful, and sincere. And know when to bail out of a losing proposition. This way you preserve your good mood and can better serve your next customer.

The Eternal Scales Are Tipped in Your Favor

Do you remember the candy-store owners at the beginning of this chapter? The more successful one knew how to tip the scales in his favor. The *eternal* scales are tipped in *your* favor because of the Law of Attraction. Something—God, Inner Management, the Universe—responds to you and supports your success.

You have a say in the kinds of experiences you have because what you think about on a regular basis tends to appear in your life. So communicate clearly with positive intent—in your interactions with people and in your advertisements—and experiment with some of the techniques discussed in this chapter. Be excited about your product, do some creative advertising, combine a willingness to be of service with a sense of adventure and fun—and expect success!

■

"Humorous advertising is doing the job. Consumers have so many distractions, so much to do, so much information clamoring for their attention, that off-beat advertising is about the only decent way of getting and holding their attention."

John Martins

■

"At that point in your life where your talent meets the needs of the world, that is where God wants you to be."

Albert Schweitzer, The Philosophy of Civilization

■

"Know the numbers and have the product information, but your sales efforts should approach an individual's mind, emotions, and funny bone. You can't reason with people who aren't paying attention."

Terry L. Paulson

■

"I don't know what your destiny will be, but one thing I do know is that the only ones among you who will be truly happy will be those who have sought and found how to serve."

Albert Schweitzer

■

"Love is a fruit in season at all times, and within reach of every hand."

Mother Teresa

■

"Everybody can be great because everybody can serve."

Martin Luther King, Jr.

■

Chapter 18

Greening Your Green
Spiritual Ways to Grow Your Profit

TRYING TO make money and be spiritual at the same
time has been a challenge," a businessman declared in a newspaper interview. Then he added, "We're a profit organization.
We can't do things out of the goodness of our hearts."

This man is successful financially. He took over a company
and parlayed its $800,000 in annual sales to $2.5 million in six
years. But he suggests that spirituality and business aren't compatible. Tell that to Sir John Marks Templeton, the mutual-fund
pioneer who merged his mutual-fund complex with Franklin
Resources for a combined $87.8 *billion* in managed assets. Over
a 33-year growth period, from 1954 to 1987, that was the largest
growth of all public investment funds in the world. Sir John, a
passionate advocate of spirituality in business, says that:

Success is rarely permanent unless it is based on ethics and
spiritual values. I would even go further and say that nothing
exists except God. Everything else is temporary, some small
manifestation of God.

Everything our investment company does to help people become more wealthy is itself a part of God's ongoing crea-

tive process. If we, therefore, try to be more in tune with God's purposes, we are more likely to help people than if we didn't understand the basic underlying reality.

Money as a Spiritual Concept

Everything in the universe is composed of the same unifying Energy or Spirit. It follows, then, that since money is part of the universe, money is also Energy or Spirit, or as Raymond Charles Barker has said, "Money is God in action"; and it should be treated as such with intelligence and respect. Knowing this, who would dare steal spiritual substance from others, waste it, engage in extortion, call people who have a lot of it 'filthy' rich, or otherwise abuse it? To mismanage or misuse money is to commit sacrilege.

What's *Your* Relationship to Money?

In a quiet, contemplative state, with a pad of paper for notes, ask yourself the following questions and notice what comes to mind.

- How do I feel about money?
- Am I comfortable with how to get money, use it, save it, invest it?
- Can I imagine myself wealthy?
- What would I do if I had a lot of money? Would I spend it? Invest it? Share it?
- Do I deserve to be rich?
- Am I willing to accept all the additional responsibilities that come with being financially successful? Do I even know what those responsibilities are?
- Am I happy when other people make a lot of money?

- Am I comfortable being with people who are more financially successful than I am?
- Would I rather inherit a large sum of money that would run out eventually than learn how to make it on my own?
- Do I have a plan to increase my wealth with deadlines to achieve each step?

Whatever your relationship to money, there are things that you can do to further increase your wealth consciousness.

10 Creative Ways to Think about Wealth

Starting right now, as you continue to read this chapter, begin to expand your awareness of true abundance.

1. Understand True Abundance

Look out the window. Do you see an end to the sky? As far out as it goes, that's how far in inner space goes. The mind reaches in all directions and has virtually no boundaries, time constraints, or limitations. Consider everything that has been discovered, invented, or thought throughout history. *Your* mind is part of the One Mind and, therefore, part of the curiosity, imagination, and creativity of the ages. It's part of the ongoing, eternal vastness. This is true abundance. And it takes infinite forms, only one of which is money.

2. Realize that You Are Everything You Need

Since you're already one with everything, you don't need anyone or anything to complete you. You're already complete, a treasure-trove of creative ideas, goals, and actions—the universe in full expression. To look outside yourself for people or things to make you feel complete is to affirm that you lack something.

And to affirm lack is to risk attracting more of it. Unity minister Carol Record adds that:

> Many of us have learned to evaluate our lives based on what we don't have. If you dwell on what you think is missing, you risk attracting more scarcity because you tend to live out your thoughts. True abundance means living your life the way you want to live it, being happy, laughing often, doing work you love, and having meaningful relationships and good health.

3. Accept that You Deserve to Be Rich

Because you are a son or daughter of Life itself, you are worthy of living the way you want to and not just getting by. It's more than okay to be rich—it's spiritually 'correct' when you do it ethically. You might want to tuck a $50 bill or a $100 bill into your wallet as an 'affirmation' and keep it there to remind yourself of this fact every time you see it.

4. Have an "Attitude of Gratitude"

If what you affirm regularly tends to manifest in your experience, then it makes sense to appreciate all the good that you already have. And you can start with yourself. Carol Record elaborates:

> What a marvelous gift you are! *You* are what you're looking for. An endless search for meaning outside yourself, often through acquiring material goods, will only wear you out. Having possessions are only one way that you can express yourself, but they won't fill you up. You're already full. You risk being disappointed when you strive for meaning outside yourself: "If only I had this product or that item or that specific relationship *then* I'd be happy." Abundance

isn't something you get, it's something you *are*, something you tune in to like tuning a radio to a particular station. If it's not tuned in properly, you'll get static, noise, and confusion.

Learn to be happy with yourself and excited about life. Have you ever seen people interviewed in the media after having survived a disaster of some sort, such as a tornado, earthquake, or flood? You've probably heard many of them say that they think they were spared because they still have something important to do in life or something to contribute. Many also report that they have a new appreciation for their loved ones and a higher regard for beauty and nature. But why wait for a fire, an avalanche, or a mudslide to appreciate these things? What happens if you're not 'fortunate' enough to experience a natural disaster? Would you go through life not knowing that you've got something important to do during your time here on the planet?

You woke up this morning! That should be sign enough that you still have important things to do here on Earth. You *are* important, disaster or no disaster. You are necessary. You are part of things. The same is true of other people too. They have important things to do, thoughts to express, dreams to fulfill, goals to achieve. So expand your appreciation of yourself and others, your experiences, and the world about you, and you'll feel more connected to Life with all its marvelous diversity and abundance.

The Bible advises us to seek first the kingdom of Heaven and all things will be added unto us. 'Heaven' can refer to the state of consciousness in which you sense your true identity, your unity with a Greater/Inner Power. And out of that sense of awe and power and reverence—from that position of strength and confidence—comes the wisdom to make the choices that will make you happy, prosperous, and fulfilled.

5. Realize that You Are More than Your Bank Account

Guard against determining your self-worth by how much money you make or have. Fortunes can come and go and come again, so it's irrational to base your self-esteem on whether you have money at a particular time in your life. Your value as a human being is a constant, regardless of temporary circumstances.

For a long time I felt good about myself only when I made money in one of two ways: as an author or as a professional speaker. The stock market could go through the roof and I'd be thrilled because I own stock, but that success didn't make me feel better about myself as a human being.

Another silly thing I used to do was put a time limit on how long I'd feel successful after I'd earned a paycheck, made either as a writer or a speaker. If I didn't receive a certain amount of money made a particular way within a specific time frame, I'd worry and get anxious and irritable. What crazy conditions I'd set on prosperity! It's a wonder that any money at all was able to make its way past my limited thinking and into my bank account! In fact, it might have made its way to me much earlier than it did—if only I'd had a healthier perspective sooner.

When I realized that abundance also included my nice house by a beautiful lake, friends, good health, and opportunities to express myself creatively, more good flowed into my life—and into my bank account. I also learned, from having had it happen so often, that my income tends to 'roller coaster' from year to year, and my financial successes often come in 'plops.' This is because I'm self-employed and continuously exploring new ways to be creative and prosperous. Since I've worked through my damaging attitudes about money, I can now relax and simply do the work I enjoy. And the money comes.

6. Examine the Language You Use to Describe Your Situation

The language that you use regarding money can help you to create a wealth consciousness—or undermine it—because wealth is more a state of mind than a state of bank account.

I've heard people declare that they're 'poor' or speak of themselves as 'indigents.' There's a sense of resignation and helplessness in these statements. And when they approach their financial woes from such a weakened state, they tend to get more of what they have.

I've also heard parents scold their children: "No, you can't have that! What do you think I'm made of—money?" In these cases, the parents missed an opportunity to instill a healthy attitude in their children by saying something like, "This was a slow year—next year should be better; maybe there's a way we [or you] can earn some extra money to buy what you want" or "Instead of buying that in a store, let's see how creative we can be and make something like it." Each of these responses suggests that a particular financial situation is temporary and that there are solutions to a problem. It gives children a greater sense of power and encourages their creativity.

When I was little, in the days when children used to go door-to-door trick-or-treating at Halloween, my mother told me to call out, "Help the poor!" instead of "Trick-or-treat!" Trick-or-treat implied that I might do something nasty to people if they didn't give me a treat. I agreed with her, but at the same time, something in me, even at that early age, resisted referring to myself as poor. I didn't feel poor. I didn't need people's help. I just wanted some candy! So I alternately called out, "Help the poor" and something more to my liking: "Happy Halloween!"

Some people think of themselves as poor, while others simply think of themselves as being 'between fortunes.' Those 'between fortunes' tend to rally faster from financial misfortune than those who are 'poor.' Then there are other people who are jealous of rich people. This kind of thinking can hold them back from achieving their own success. It's important to have a positive attitude about people who have money—especially if you want to be one of them!

Author and entrepreneur Zig Ziglar shares the following insights about money:

> I believe that so long as money doesn't become your god, you're morally obligated to earn large amounts of it. A lot of people don't have much money because they don't understand it. They talk about "cold, hard cash." It's neither cold nor hard. It's soft and warm and it feels good. It's a worthy goal. I don't believe that you can get too much money, but I believe if the money gets you, you've got a problem.

7. Prepare to Have Money

Are you mentally prepared to receive large sums of money? In my own experience, I affirmed abundance, thought up lots of money-making ideas, and regularly wrote about success. But I was caught off guard when success actually came and large amounts of money started rolling in from my best-selling audio-cassette album.

I was clueless about investing and didn't know what to do with all the extra money after my bills were paid. So I just deposited it in a checking/savings account in a local bank, which paid minimum interest. I was a fast study, fortunately, and quickly learned better ways to make the most of my money.

So it's a good idea to figure out how you'd manage a large sum of money before you're actually called on to do so. If you haven't already learned the basic concepts of good money-management, you might want to educate yourself. An easy way to do this is to start reading magazines and newsletters that relate to managing money.

It's also smart to respect the money you already have by

managing it well. Be sure that your records are up to date so you can analyze, monitor, and validate your financial condition. You'll also want your paperwork in order, checkbook balanced, and credit rating good. If you hire someone to organize your finances for you, such as a bookkeeper or an accountant, be sure to have enough financial savvy to oversee the people you hire. Having your financial affairs in order is an excellent affirmation that you're ready to receive an increase.

8. Explore New Ways to Make Money

Are you content with a regular paycheck? That's perfectly fine, but realize that a paycheck is only one way you can make money. Your imagination can be your most powerful tool for opening doors to money-making opportunities. Here's a technique to spark your creativity to think of new money-making opportunities:

Each week list 20 new ways to make money. Welcome all the ideas that you have, regardless of how impractical they may seem. This will help you 'break out of the box' of traditional, limited thinking. Seemingly crazy or impractical ideas might give rise to something totally unexpected that actually might work.

After you've completed the list, narrow it down by asking which ideas you'd be willing to spend 15 minutes a day developing. If you aren't willing to spend even a minimum amount of time on a particular idea, move to the next one.

When you've chosen an idea you'd like to explore further, organize it on paper, break it into steps, and set time limits on when you want to accomplish each step. Be aware of any resistance that you experience. It may be that as soon as you get serious about a project, you get scared of the commitment, the responsibility, or the effort involved. At this point, decide if you really want to follow through with that particular idea. If not, move to another one.

Be sure, at this initial stage, to keep your day job. It's probably a good idea to work part-time on your money-making ideas until they become lucrative enough to support you—if that's what you want. Or you might want just enough money to supplement the income you're already making from your regular job.

9. Give 'till It Helps

When you change your focus from how well you're doing—financially, socially, and professionally—to how you can contribute something of value to others, amazing things begin to happen.

David Dunn, author of *Try Giving Yourself Away*, writes: "Giving away rids the system of selfishness, and produces a healthy glow that warms the spirit."

A professional speaker told me that one way she learned to stop feeling self-conscious onstage was to focus on giving to her audience. "I used to worry about how I looked up there," she said. "Was my makeup appropriate, my suit in style, my hair behaving itself? And how was I doing? Did I sound intelligent? Would these people ask me back again?

"I'd work myself into such a nervous state that I had to do something to preserve my sanity. Finally instead of focusing on myself, I switched my focus to my audience. Were they having fun? Were they learning? What could I do to put them at ease and make them feel comfortable? How could I make their day more positive and productive? As a result of my change in focus, I now have all the business I want."

A businessman told me that he used to make unwise investments and lose money every time. He confided that he felt uncomfortable having a lot of money because so many people had less. He thought that he might be sabotaging his success. I knew that he was a compassionate person, so I pointed out that he could do more good for people by *having* money than by not having it. He agreed, examined his attiutdes about money, and began to invest in more stable ventures. Today he's doing very well financially and loves to share his business acumen with others and help them get rich too.

Giving seems to have a cumulative effect. The more you do it, the better you feel. And the better you feel, the more open you are to even more prosperity. Chapter 20, "From Go-Giver to Go-Getter," gives you 30 more ideas on giving.

10. Socially Responsible Investing

Whenever you invest money, your investment has consequences: socially, ethically, and sometimes globally. You therefore might want to align your financial goals with your values and invest in a socially responsible fund. These funds have 'social screens'—nonfinancial criteria that are used to analyze a company's suitability to be included in a portfolio. Such a fund might invest in companies that:

- produce only life-affirming products and services
- have existing or emerging technologies that enhance social development
- don't make money from gambling, tobacco, alcohol, or weapons
- have fair employment policies
- have sound environmental practices
- respect human rights

Nonfinancial dividends that you can attribute to your investment might be increased employment, reduced pollution, low-income housing development, or better health care.

You can research the socially repsonsible funds by reading the current fiancial magazines in bookstores or libraries. Before you invest, though, call a fund and ask for its prospectus to make sure that it's the best one for you. You'll also want to compare it to the other funds available so that you know your options. And, because these funds may not be federally insured, never bet the rent money.

6.5 Million Millionaires

It's estimated that in the year 2000, there will be 6.5 *million* millionaires in the United States. Could *you* be one of them? Anything is possible in a universe of infinite possibilities. At this writing, there are 121 billionaires! Care to make it 122?

Money is neither good nor bad; it just *is*. And put in the proper perspective, it can enhance your life and the lives of others.

It has been said that "the rich get richer." This means that when you're rich in mind and heart, imagination and attitude, you'll be a natural at attracting money. You'll see possibilities and opportunities instead of obstacles, have plenty of money-making ideas, and be more generous with others. You'll give your best and you'll get the best. You'll be rich beyond measure.

■

"It is not he who has little but he who always wants more who is poor."

Seneca

■

"Wealth does not consist of having great possessions, but having few desires."

Epicurus, Fragments

■

"I never saw a U-Haul behind a hearse."

Reverend Billy Graham

■

"The thing to try when all else fails is: again."

Author Unknown

■

"It's not how much we have but how much we enjoy that makes us happy."

Author Unknown

■

"We begin each of our stockholders' meetings with a prayer. But we certainly don't pray that the investments we made yesterday will go up today. . . . we pray for wisdom, for understanding, and for an open mind to God's will. We pray that our direction will benefit all parties involved."

Sir John Marks Templeton, founder of
The Templeton Growth Fund

■

"There is no wealth but life."

John Ruskin

■

Chapter 19

Success at Last
Help for the New Arrivals

NOW YOU'VE done it. You've expected the best, affirmed prosperity and abundance for yourself and the people with whom you work, done your job with integrity, given thanks for all you have, and kept a spiritual perspective at the office—and it's worked! Your life keeps getting better. Something eternal has responded to you, and every day you prove that "Nothing succeeds like success."

You've spent most of your life so far getting somewhere. The quest is all you've known. But now you're finally where you've been wanting to get. You have the job you want, the salary, the prestige, the recognition. You have arrived.

Now What?

Are you happy and enjoying life to the fullest? Or are you like many people who go through a period of adjustment to being successful? Let's eavesdrop on the comments of a few new arrivals:

- Is this too good to be true? Do I deserve all this good fortune?
- I feel a letdown. I got the promotion I wanted so much. Now I need another goal.
- I've just traded in my old problems for new ones.
- What if something terrible happens and I lose it all?
- I'm a little embarrassed by how successful I've become. I feel uncomfortable having it so good when so many people have less.
- It took me a while to realize that I'd achieved my financial goals. I'm making enough interest income on my principal that I don't have to work if I don't want to. I've been so used to trying to make as much money as I could that I passed the income level most people consider wealthy. It didn't even occur to me to stop for a while and take a breather.
- I've crossed the line between being a high achiever and an overachiever. There are increasing demands on my time, energy, and talent. I say "Yes" to more and more opportunities and "Can do" to more and more people, and now I've overextended myself. I try to do too many things at a time and have trouble turning off work at the end of the day.

As a new arrival to success you've proven how powerful you are. You've achieved success by setting goals, having a mission and a vision, and working diligently. Now it's important to keep moving forward with calm assurance.

You Deserve Success

Remember that as a spiritual being, it's your birthright to be happy, healthy, rich, and prosperous. When you achieve success ethically, wealth is spiritual philosophy fulfilled. You've worked diligently and creatively. You've expected the best and, in doing so, you've created a corresponding equivalent in your outer experience. You've done your spiritual homework. Enjoy the benefits.

Now You Need a New Goal

Some people report feeling a letdown when they finally achieve their goal, whether it's financial, social, or career-oriented. That's their adrenaline levels returning to normal. They're no longer living on the edge. Their ingenuity and perseverance are no longer being tested. They may feel that the thrill of the quest is over. But success automatically spawns the need for new goals. Now you may have to learn new skills such as how to delegate, manage greater sums of money, communicate more effectively, expand your market, and keep it all going comfortably.

You're playing on a higher level. If you're the boss or the business owner, you may have worried at one time about how you were going to keep the business open, the lights on, and the bills paid. Now that you've met those basic needs, you have new opportunities such as enlarging your customer/client base, meeting an ever-increasing demand for your product or service, and exploring ways to share your good fortune.

If you're an employee, now that you've achieved the recognition, promotion, or raise that you wanted, you might feel pressured to continue to live up to other people's expectations.

Whether you're an employer or employee, you became successful by being confident, creative, and resourceful. Now embark on any new challenges with all the customary enthusiasm, savvy, and talent that you used to achieve your earlier goals. And continue to grow spiritually.

You Have the Formula

Fortunes may come and go and come again. You've proven that you have the flexibility, the skills, and the perseverance to succeed. Remember that circumstances are temporary. What remains constant is your personal connection with Spirit. Use that connection to help you to weather difficulties, meet challenges, and get ahead. You have the formula for success. Use it.

Success as a Tool

You can use your success to help promote or finance worthy causes. If this is something you'd like to do, here's a list of causes that you might want to consider:

Save the oceans or rain forests	Help the homeless or hungry
Support AIDS research	Support animal rights
Combat drug abuse	Help sick children
Help overcome illiteracy	Support hospice programs

If you have a computer, a quick way to find information regarding these causes, and the associations that support them, is to go online on the Internet, go into a search engine, and do a search according to the stated protocol for that particular search engine. If you don't have a computer, you could start at your local library. Look in the *Encyclopedia of Associations* or ask the reference librarian for help.

For more ideas on how to make your success count, read the next chapter, "From Go-Getter to Go-Giver."

Overachiever or High Achiever?

The world needs achievers like you, the 'movers and shakers.' That's how humanity makes progress. And yet, high achievers often run the risk of becoming *over*achievers by taking on too much, by focusing on what they have left to do rather than celebrating what they've already done. And in doing so, they may put themselves in danger of burnout.

Do you ever postpone activities that have no deadlines, but which give your life value and meaning, such as a social life, meditation, exercise, and leisure time?

There's usually no deadline on friendships or spending time with your family, so you might be tempted to let these valuable relationships slide.

Meditating is another activity that you might be tempted to put on hold if you've overscheduled yourself professionally. This is unfortunate, because meditation, often instrumental in helping you to stay emotionally and intellectually balanced enough to become successful in the first place, can help you to continue to stay mentally well balanced when your business life gets hectic.

Or maybe you procrastinate on exercising, rationalizing that you'll exercise twice as hard next week when you're less busy. But exercise is something that you need to do on a regular basis to enjoy the benefits.

Or maybe you defer leisure time to fill your day with more and more activity. As an overachiever, you might find it a real challenge to sit still long enough to meditate or to relax, but it's good to take a break before you feel you need one.

Preventing burnout is easier than trying to recover from it once it has happened. Spending time with friends will energize you. Spending regular quiet time with yourself will refresh you. Balancing work with leisure will help keep you healthy.

Put the Call Through

Make time to attend to what's truly important in your life. How do you feel when you telephone someone and you're put on hold? You probably don't like it. So why put *yourself* on hold when you feel a need to read an inspirational book, get in touch with a friend, or take a well-deserved break? I doubt that your Soul enjoys being put on hold. You'll feel much better if you 'put the call through.'

Stop postponing what you need to do to keep spiritually fit. Schedule time for meditating, family, friends, classes, inspirational or entertaining reading, and relaxing.

Begin today to achieve a balance between work and leisure or you may end up with no support system at all. Here are 10 ideas on how to keep the foundation strong:

1. Realize that the measure of success is not always a hefty bank account. Being successful can also mean having good friends and a supportive family, having a job you like, being able to express your creativity, or having leisure time.
2. Clarify your valued objectives and set realistic goals to keep you on target in your personal and professional life.
3. Take care of your health, be good to yourself. Take breaks and vacations. Meditate regularly.
4. Limit the number of projects you take on at a time.
5. Free up your schedule by delegating items and activities, such as cleaning, yard work, office work, research, and making sales calls.
6. Look forward to learning new skills. Be curious about what tomorrow will bring.
7. Be assertive. Say "No" occasionally, or "Not now, maybe later."
8. Expand your personal and professional networks.

9. Replace any concerns you have with gentle reminders to yourself of how well your life is working. Be thankful for, and celebrate, all that you've accomplished so far.
10. Look for ways to share your good fortune with others.

When you build your accomplishments on a solid spiritual foundation, you'll move from win to win, and your successes will have staying-power.

■

"Half an hour's meditation is essential, except when you are very busy. Then a full hour is needed."

St. Francis de Sales

■

"We shall be remembered more for our kindnesses than for our accomplishments, for our generosity than for our riches, and for our service than for our success."

Bill Ward

■

"You make a living with what you get, but you make a life with what you give."

Author Unknown

■

Chapter 20

From "Go-Getter" to "Go-Giver"

Success is often achieved by entrepreneurs working diligently against all odds to make a 'go' of their business, CEOs sacrificing their relationships or leisure time to build a company, and employees trying to make a difference and make their 'mark' in an organization by working overtime, evenings, and weekends. In the beginning, many of us operate out of a self-centered, survival mode while learning the ropes. But eventually, those of us who persevere get good at what we do.

Once we feel confident that we can meet our basic needs, we're free to move from a survival-based consciousness to a more socially based consciousness. This can lead to a kind of success that's more gratifying and more enduring: contributing something of value to others and to the world.

Giving Changes the Game

Ernest Holmes reminds us that "It is only when we allow the Divine current to flow through us on and out, that we really express life."

An example of this idea is the Dead Sea, which is called "dead" because water only flows into it—there's no outflow. Likewise, we run the risk of stagnating at a particular level in life, even at a particular level of success, if we don't keep things circulating.

We can keep things moving and make our success count for something when we understand it in relation to what we do with it. For example, $1000 is simply $1000; but it takes on new meaning if it's used constructively to help finance someone's education, feed the hungry, or preserve the environment. Likewise, an hour is just an hour; but it has greater meaning if it's used to help others in some way.

When we have a purpose about which to be enthused, our success means something in terms of the world in which we live, and we feel more connected with the natural flow of the universe.

Recognize What You've Already Given

List all the ways that you've already served others, such as helping to fight illiteracy, being a good role model, donating money to your favorite charity, or being a good friend and listening when someone needed to talk. Then look for opportunities to do these activities on a more regular basis and to expand the various ways that you serve the business community and the world in general. Whether you were a "go-giver" from the beginning of your career or you're only now ready to transform yourself into a "go-giver," here are 30 ideas to consider:

Give to the Source of Your Inspiration

1. Tithe to your church, synagogue, teacher, friend, association, or a particular place that stirs your soul by encouraging, inspiring, and enlightening you. A tithe, typically 10 percent of one's income, is an affirmation that God is the true source of supply: ideas, income, abundance, and opportunities. If you have more than one source of inspiration, you might want to distribute your tithe between them.

Give to Yourself

2. Impress upon yourself the unending abundance in the universe. Enjoy a facial, a massage, a movie, a good book, a class, a hobby, a subscription to a favorite magazine, a bubble bath, an exotic vacation, a meal with a friend, a weekend at a spa, a party, a walk in the forest or by a lake, gardening, boating, writing, painting, dancing, playing or watching sports, spending time with your family, children, or pets. Whatever gives you pleasure. Life is meant to be enjoyed!

Give Time, Talent, or Inspiration

3. Share your knowledge, enthusiasm, or experience. For example, you might want to work with, and inspire, career-oriented teenagers.
4. If you're retired you might consider being a consultant for the Small Business Association, which provides specialized information and services to the business community throughout the United States.
5. Set up an apprenticeship program in your company for someone to learn the business.
6. Give someone a needed reference, a lead, a contact, or an important telephone number that could help his or her career.
7. Inspire and encourage those coming up through the ranks. Join professional organizations or associations to identify special needs within your field.
8. If you're a supervisor, manager, or boss, delegate opportunity as well as responsibility.
9. Recognize the good work that people do at the company. Put your praise and commendations in writing for their personnel files.

10. Remember what's important to your customers, clients, and co-workers, such as certain values, birthdays, hobbies, special occasions, or the names of their family members.
11. Give intangibles, such as leadership, loyalty, enthusiasm, creativity, or patience.
12. Use any fame, fortune, or influence that you have to promote causes in which you believe, such as fighting the use of dangerous pesticides on food, combating drug abuse, or helping the homeless.

Give to the Environment

13. Give back when you take something. If you're a publisher, for example, plant a tree every time you go to press.
14. If you're a consumer, do business with environmentally conscious companies.
15. If you're a manufacturer or office-worker, reduce energy consumption and recycle paper, plastics, and other appropriate material.

Give Money

16. Invest in socially responsible funds.
17. Donate a percentage of your income or profits to worthy causes (see Chapter 19 for some ideas).
18. Set up a scholarship fund for young people who are interested in learning your profession.
19. Establish a sliding scale for payment so that people with less money can still benefit from your goods or services.
20. Have special discounts for nonprofit organizations, schools, and students.
21. Be willing to negotiate for your product or services. Give quantity discounts and price breaks.

Give Thanks

22. Carry stamped postcards with you for writing quick thank-you notes as you go about your daily business.

23. Buy a 'thank-you' stamp to stamp the checks you use to pay bills. Instead of cursing your bills, be glad that you have the money to pay them. In restaurants, when it's time for the check, rather than asking, "What's the damage?" be happy that you can afford to eat in a restaurant.

24. Say "thanks" to people at work by honoring them at business lunches or award banquets.

25. Write letters of appreciation to people whose work you admire.

26. Say "Hi" or "Welcome" with flowers or a note to new businesses in your area.

27. Congratulate your 'competitors' for landing important clients. After all, they're out there diligently helping to create a market for your product.

28. Thank the people who helped you along the way to success: teachers, mentors, families, friends, co-workers, customers, and clients.

29. Remember the 'unsung heroes' in your professional life: people who deliver your mail and packages on time, friendly storekeepers, people who repair and maintain the office equipment, helpful secretaries and receptionists who answer your questions, and anyone who comes to the job regularly, cheerfully, and on time to be there for you.

30. Be generous and specific with your praise. People love to hear how well they're doing.

Give Now

You're invited to join a worldwide giving spree. When you finish reading this book, give something to someone. Thank an employee, your boss, the staff, a manager, a supervisor, or a valued customer. Give a compliment, a gift, an award, a smile, or a pleasant word. Give something of your time, talent, money, knowledge, or humor. Then notice how good you feel. And also notice that when you give your best, you *get* the best.

■

"Real generosity toward the future consists in giving all to what is present."

Albert Camus

■

"Give what you have. To someone, it may be better than you dare to think."

Henry Wadsworth Longfellow

■

"If I can stop one heart from breaking, I shall not live in vain."

Emily Dickinson, "Life"

■

"Everything flows out and in; everything has its tides."

The Kybalion

■

"The meaning of good and bad, of better and worse, is simply helping or hurting."

Ralph Waldo Emerson

■

Open for Business

WHEN YOU do your job from a spiritual perspective, 'Open for Business' takes on new meaning. It means that you're open to the spiritual reality of who you are and why you're here: to enjoy love and prosperity, give love, live creatively with enthusiasm, contribute something of value to others, and continue to evolve spiritually. It means that you're open to receive, experience, and give.

Because business is spiritual in character, it grows, changes, and makes progress, just as the people involved grow, change, and make progress. When you use spiritual principles at work and think of the office as your 'church' or your 'temple,' you'll be calmer, more inner-directed, and less affected by circumstances. You'll think more clearly, make better decisions, and attract positive people. You'll invite experiences that nurture and further your spiritual growth. You'll know that there's a Power for good in your life, and with this Power available to you, you can do anything.

Today, well lived,
makes yesterday a dream of happiness
and tomorrow a vision of hope.
Sanskrit saying

Index

Kathleen Hawkins is vice president of the National Management Institute, in the Dallas/Fort Worth area, and the author of four books, *Time Management Made Easy*, *Test Your Entrepreneurial IQ*, *Reverse Speech: Hidden Messages in Human Communication*, and *Spirit Incorporated*. She wrote a column for five years for *Success* magazine and wrote and produced the best-selling audio-cassette programs *Speed Read to Win* and *How to Organize Yourself to Win*. Her articles and ideas on how to increase personal and professional effectiveness have appeared in more than 200 publications. She's also a reading specialist—with master's degrees in reading education and creative writing—and a professional speaker and a business consultant. Thousands of people from all levels of business, science, education, and industry have taken her courses. She's been using a spiritual perspective in business as long as she has been in business.

Endorsements for **Spirit Incorporated**

"Kathleen Hawkins provides readers with meaningful, practical techniques for applying life-affirming principles to their everyday work lives."

JOHN E. RENESCH
Editor, *Leadership in a New Era*

"Kathleen Hawkins takes the mystery out of the relationship between business and spirituality. Her use of analogy makes it easy for the reader to connect with the principles and incorporate them into the workplace. Her practical tips can be easily implemented. She shows how the frequent insanity of business can be transformed into a more sane, nurturing, and productive venture."

SUSAN PILGRIM, Ph.D.
author of *Living InSync -- Creating Your*
Life with Balance and Purpose

"A treasury of practical ideas built on universal spiritual principles that anyone can use at work. What a find!"

PATRICE KARST
author of *God Made Easy*

"Something for everyone! This book provides many touchstones for anyone thinking about how to make their work and spiritual life compatible. Every page is filled with stimulating thoughts that can change your thinking and motivate new behaviors."

STEWART L. LEVINE
author of *Getting to Resolution*